GW00643571

One Hundred Hints
for Better Betting

AP

AESCULUS
PRESS LTD

www.bestbetbooks.co.uk

Cover by Pure Design, Shrewsbury

Aesculus Press Limited
PO Box 170
Nantwich
Cheshire
CW5 6WX

Typeset on an Apple Macintosh
by Aesculus Press using QuarkXpress

Printed and bound in Great Britain by Ashford Colour Press Ltd.,
Gosport, Hants.

1-904328-11-3

publisher's note

This book is a reprint and, a design alteration and the occasional typographical change apart, has been reproduced in its original 1994 form - including now outdated references, for example, to betting tax. The reasons for retaining these and similar references will, we trust, become self-evident as you read further.

about the author

Mark Coton turned down the chance to become a barrister in order to pursue what he hesitates to describe as a career in betting. Having worked for *Trainers Record* and Ladbrokes, he first came to prominence during his four years at the *Racing Post*, when he formulated and developed the highly successful Pricewise concept, as well as speaking out on behalf of punters in his *Better Betting* column. Mark wrote his best-selling book *Value Betting* after leaving the *Racing Post* in January 1990 and has since returned to the law by teaching part-time at the University of North London. In September 1991 he became chairman of the National Association for the Protection of Punters and has contributed to many publications both in that capacity and, after stepping down from the role, as a journalist. Mark's main form of relaxation is drinking the fine wine he purchased in bulk after Nashwan won the 2,000 Guineas and Derby in 1989.

acknowledgements

The author would like to thank, among the many who have encouraged and at times had to put up with my betting over the years, Charles and Yu Finch, David and Philippa Ikerrin, John Lefley, Ed Linfoot, Andrew Munro, Jonathan Ramsden, Simon Stanley, Emily Weber, Vivienne West, John White and Terry Woods.

The book is dedicated to my parents, Gordon and Maureen,
for all their love and support over the years

contents

introduction   11

part one   **betting like a professional)**   **14**

a cautionary tale   15

part two   **the one hundred hints**   **20**

stage one   **a fresh start**   21

stage two   **making selections**   27

stage three   **assessing values**   63

stage four   **preparing to bet**   79

stage five   **staking**   91

stage six   **the result**   105

stage seven   **winding down**   109

stage eight   **taking stock**   111

stage nine   **betting for a living**   127

part three   **the top ten hints**   **136**

stage ten   **the conclusion**   137

10 . one hundred hints

introduction

This book has been written with one leading assumption in mind - that the reader, like the author, wishes to profit more from his or her betting. To profit not just financially, though this will clearly be an overriding consideration, but also in terms of the enjoyment and satisfaction gained from the betting process. There appears to be an easy formula to hand here. If you win more, you are going to gain more enjoyment and satisfaction. No doubt. But for the purposes of this book, I am going to reverse the formula and argue that if you get more enjoyment and satisfaction from your betting, you are going to win more in the long run. Not that this turnaround will be at all easy to achieve. Far from it. For every punter who aims to bet profitably has to undertake the long and cheerless task of identifying and then rooting out all the bad habits which have been costing them dear.

Writing the book has helped me undertake this process and, painful though it has been, I can assure you it has been worthwhile. After 15 years of serious betting, I now feel more confident than ever about my ability to beat the bookmaker and beat him well. Although I had enjoyed some great success with my betting, notably during 1989 when a £20,000 coup on Nashwan was the highlight of an astonishing summer, I was aware that I had by no means mastered the system. This was proved the very next summer when I endured a devastating sequence of 49 losers.

In the spring of 1993, I decided to try to tackle the game head-on, by setting myself up as a professional punter for the six months from the Newmarket Craven Meeting in April to the Cesarewitch in October. The project was a failure.

Not only did I lose a good deal of money, but I found myself making elementary mistakes, the sort of mistakes I should have rooted out a decade ago. Far from being enjoyable, the summer was frustrating and deeply unfulfilling. Indeed, I stopped betting altogether in the middle of August, fed up at my results and the run of bad luck I had been enduring.

Taking this break was one of the best decisions I have ever taken. After 15 years of almost continuous betting, I was finally able to take a relaxed perspective about the game. I realise now that a sense of composure and detachment was precisely what I lacked when it came to betting. I was a good judge of the form book and of value - of that there was no doubt. But my betting had always lacked consistency, being dogged by haphazard staking and always vulnerable to mood swings which could pitch from elation to dejection within a week. It is my guess that many other punters would have to hold up their hands and admit to similar feelings.

As a result, you will find this book is as much about developing discipline and detachment as it is about refining winner-finding technique and developing methods for value appraisal. (These issues are addressed in greater detail in my earlier book, *Value Betting*.) If we are not careful the betting process becomes a chaotic blur. Decisions are taken at random to no particular purpose, encouraged by the helter-skelter atmosphere in the ring or the betting shop.

To paraphrase Robert Pirsig in *Zen And The Art Of Motorcycle Maintenance*, we're so busy looking for a winner that if a winner came knocking at the door we'd say, "Go away, I'm looking for a winner." Many punters go through their entire betting lives without once taking stock of their actions. This would be fine and understandable if these punters enjoyed their betting, but 20 minutes spent in a betting shop or racecourse ring suggests that few actually do. The stock expressions are frowns, grimaces and shakes of the head. Betting slips are angrily torn or screwed up and projected across the room.

As I have admitted, I did not enjoy the summer of 1993 greatly myself. Of 85 bets struck, only seven were winners, a particularly poor strike-rate even for one who was tending to back in the 8-1+ region. Almost everything that could go wrong did go wrong and many of the disasters litter the pages of this book. It would have been easy to curse the gambling gods, to blame it all on luck, but this would have missed the point entirely. Luck had not come into it. I had got no more than I had deserved.

After a two-month break, I printed out the year's bets and began to analyse them. I reviewed my diary. I made a list of mistakes made, faults exposed and opportunities missed. The list of these faults and missed opportunities began to extend so far, I realised there was enough material for a book on them. Not the sort of book I had been hoping to write at the start of the previous summer, which was to be one full of decisive decision-making, of shrewd and heavily-backed winners, and of evenings spent sipping champagne on the lawns of luxury hotels.

A book, by contrast, which would be introspective, perhaps to a fault, yet rigorous and honest. One which would hopefully clear the fog surrounding our betting and enable us to approach the game keen, refreshed and full of a rare sense of purpose.

I have always had a deep conviction that the game can be beaten, and beaten well, and that conviction has been strengthened by writing this book. I hope that your convictions, whatever they are, will be strengthened too, and that you find much to entertain in the pages to come.

part one
betting like a professional

a cautionary tale

Before we attack the 100 hints, here is an imaginary scenario to test your reflexes as a backer. Imagine you are sitting in a pub, enjoying your first quiet drink of the evening. A ruddy, corpulent gentleman has been chatting with the barman and pointing none too discreetly in your direction. He comes over. You immediately recognise him as an old-style bookmaker, with loud check jacket, half-smoked cigar and an overbearing manner. Such a contrast, you feel, to the faceless accountants who run the big betting firms with all the flair and charm of an old-style KGB agent.

"I've a little proposition for you," says the bookmaker, taking a seat at your table. "A simple toss of the coin."

Some readers may recognise this figure and his propositions from chapter one of *Value Betting*. Perhaps you will feel there is something of a score to settle with him. "I'm going to offer you 6-4 heads," says the bookmaker, idly tossing an immaculate gold coin into the air. "What do you reckon?"

You take a long sip at your drink, evaluating the proposition, and not without suspicion. The odds are so favourable you are half-expecting Tom Kelly of BOLA to appear, grim-faced, from behind one of the potted plants to call an immediate inquiry.

So what is your response? Try to think of all the angles, all the options. If your immediate reaction is to call for the biggest bet you can afford before rushing to the nearest cash dispenser for the maximum withdrawal, you can certainly be classed as a gambler - but it's a fair shade of odds-on your hotheadedness has got you into trouble on more than one occasion in the past.

Tonight you are in luck, because another figure approaches and introduces himself as a professional gambler. You look him up and down and are reassured by his confident body language - eyes sharp and alert, though hinting at a certain coldness. You ask him to take a seat. As he does so he takes a critical look at your near-finished pint. He is drinking orange juice himself and will tell you later, when the business is done, that there is at least one golden rule in this game: never drink and gamble.

The professional looks at the bookmaker, whose jovial manner appears to have retreated. Perhaps he remembers closing the professional's account earlier in the summer having noted some 'unusual betting patterns'.

"First thing," says the professional, taking over, "is never trust a bookmaker, certainly those who go touting for business in places like these. Let's have a look at that coin." The bookmaker shrugs his shoulders and hands it over to the professional, who inspects it and lays it down on the table. "Let's keep it in sight at all times," he orders, before asking for the odds."6-4 heads," confirms the bookmaker.

"Right. Now this is the critical question," says the professional, turning to make sure you are retaining your concentration. "How many spins have we got?"

"Let's say 10," replies the bookmaker.

"OK. The way I see it is this," continues the professional, with impressive speed. "You've a margin here of 25 per cent. That's the profit we can reasonably expect on 10 spins, although it's not much of sample. If you win four out of 10, for instance, you're only going to break even. Of course if you lose, you're just going to shake your head and walk away as if nothing had happened."

You nod in confirmation. Things suddenly seem a whole lot more complicated, but at least this professional knows what he's talking about, or so it would seem.

"What's your bank then?" asks the professional.

You just manage to stop yourself saying "Barclays" before reaching for your wallet. "Cash, no credit," says the bookmaker.

You have one hundred pounds, which you place on the table. It looks rather vulnerable lying there, despite the attractiveness of the proposition.

"How are you going to play it then?" asks the professional.

You ponder the options. Clearly it would be reckless to risk all on one spin when 10 are offered. Fifty pounds on the first spin and the other £50 on the next if you lose on the first? You look at the professional, but there is no great encouragement to be gleaned from his expression as he quietly sips his orange juice. You decide to play safe. "I'm going to have £10 on each spin. It's reasonable to expect to win five out of 10 and thus draw a profit of £25, which is the margin in my favour," you reply.

The professional nods slowly. "I'm not going to argue with that," he says. "But, before we start, tell me one thing. How are you feeling?"

"Fine," you reply, certain that your voice has betrayed surprise at the question.

"About the bet. Come on. How do you feel inside? Confident? Uneasy?"

"To be honest..."

"You should never be anything else, especially with yourself," interrupts the professional.

"As I was saying, to be honest, I was looking forward to a bit of a crack when our friend here first came over, but now my head is full of figures and I don't know which way to turn."

"That's good," replies the professional unexpectedly. At this point you cannot help but think he is beginning to muddy the waters.

"One of the secrets of this game is to feel composed and confident. 'At home' is my expression for it," continues the professional. "Believe me, when you feel like this you cannot go wrong. And this little bet our friend is offering has been rather instructive. Because you cannot feel 'at home' if your head is a jumble of figures and your mind is in a spin about how much to put on. Are you with me?"

You nod, but cannot entirely suppress the desire to leave this one-way conversation trailing behind as you go to the bar for another pint.

"There's no substitute for doing your homework. In this case it means knowing the odds and percentages. If you're betting on horses, it means checking the form of all the runners, asking whether the ground will suit, and the trip, maybe the draw, if the trainer is in form - that kind of thing. You gather this information in your mind and reach a decision about which horses you are interested in for the race. Then you leave all that thinking behind, confident you have considered all the angles, ready to concentrate on the next task, which is considering the price.

"The importance is not to get yourself into a fluster. Just look at some guys in the betting shop. They've picked out a horse and are about to back it, then they notice another is being backed. Next thing they are rushing to the paper to see who trains it, what it did last time, and so on. You will know all of those things and will not have to waste any time worrying about the supported horse. Maybe you can say to yourself, 'I'm not interested in this horse because it is unproven on the ground.' Of course, while the others are checking on this supposed gamble, the price for their fancy shortens too. Then they are in yet another fluster, unsure of how much to have on at the new price. Then it shortens another point and it is a pound to penny they end up having more on their original fancy at a much shorter price than they could and should have taken. That's how things go wrong in this game."

You nod again, no doubt from experience.

"Right, so you've done your homework. Then you consider the price you are likely to get and the amount you wish to stake. People forget that betting involves three important processes - the evaluation of form, the evaluation of price, and the staking. When you are in the ring, or in a betting shop when a show comes through, you can only afford to be concentrating on the last two. If you are on top of the game, you will have a firm idea in your mind how much you will stake on your favoured horse at a given price. So as soon as the show comes through, you are ready to step in. Or stay out if the price is too short.

Here's another common fault. A punter has picked out a horse and maybe made a good case for it. He has looked at the betting forecast in the paper and is expecting 5-1. He has a sum of money in mind to put on at that price. It shows at 7-1. The punter should now be stepping in with a bigger bet than planned, but he's actually in a fluster again because he has not considered the possibility of 7-1 showing. As he is dithering over how much to stake, the horse shortens to 5-1. Then he is furious with himself for missing the 7-1 and spends a second or two quietly cursing himself. A queue has built up at the counter. By the time he is there with his bet his horse is 4-1."

You nod again.

"Then maybe the horse goes in and instead of congratulating himself on a successful coup, he's thinking about what might have been. The regrets blur his judgement and he goes on to strike a couple more bets in the hope of winning what he should have won on the 7-1 shot. Of course these bets lose. This is how things slip away from you as a punter - and all because you have not done your homework and cleared your mind of all the doubts and niggles. 'Clear your mind' - there's another little phrase for you."

"So you asked me how I felt in order to see if I was 'at home' with this bet, or whatever you call it?" you ask.

"More or less."

"Actually I'm not sure you haven't made the whole thing so complicated, I feel like giving up. In fact, you haven't added to my confidence, you've taken it away. I know you're a professional, so you have to know these things but isn't it best for the rest of us to remain in a state of blissful ignorance? I could probably have won a fortune off our friend here by now. As it is we've been here for the best part of half an hour and I haven't struck a bet yet."

"I'm not going to pretend this game is in any way easy, but things do get easier and seem less complex when you've picked up good habits instead of all the bad ones we carry around with us. Think about the word. Habit is something you do without thinking consciously about it. Those bad habits are costing us money - and because we haven't recognised them, we don't even realise it! But, just the same, good habits can help us win. As for the point about blissful ignorance... well, I'm not dictating to anybody about the time and effort they should put into their betting. It is just that if you want to win, you owe it to yourself to get your act together. Punters spend far too much time moaning and not enough examining their technique. Don't moan, learn. That's my motto. Right, let's have these bets now."

You turn to the bookmaker, who had been sitting quietly through the whole affair, now puffing on a fresh cigar. Cuban by the smell of it.

"Before you start, I'll give one more tip," says the professional. "For me, your strategy of a tenner on each spin is a little too cautious. Strictly for the technicians, as we call them, the steady grinders who make some kind of a living from the game but lack any kind of flair. The successful gambler needs a bold, audacious streak in his make-up. Say you move up to £20 per spin. Five straight losers and you'll have done your money, but the chance of such a sequence is 31-1. I reckon we can live with that. There's always another day in this game. And every time your bank is in profit, stake one-fifth of it on the next throw. This way, if you hit a winning streak, you'll get paid a lot more than under your system. You could even begin with £25 per spin. It's up to you. Far be it from me to try to influence your decision."

At this point the professional smiles. Then he rises from his seat and makes his exit. The bookmaker takes your first stake, picks up the coin and tosses it high in the air. Before it lands, you turn to the door and the professional gives you another smile, somewhat enigmatic, before disappearing from sight. You turn to view the coin, glittering on the wooden floor. Heads. Maybe, at last, your luck is about to turn.

part two

the one hundred hints

stage **one**

a fresh start

Hint 1: Set aside a betting bank

This is the first important step in betting on a disciplined and organised basis. Open a new bank or building society account, and deposit as much money as you can afford purely for betting. If necessary, open another account for expenses on newspapers, form books, racecourse visits and other expenditure. Satisfy yourself there is enough in the account to withstand a losing run of 20 straight selections at your average stake per bet. Do not cobble together a bank with a few stray fivers and the week's drinking money. If necessary take a break from betting and save up enough to allow yourself to feel you are on solid ground.

Setting aside such a bank will give more than the impression of making a clean start - it should be treated as one. From now on, money should only be taken from this account when you are completely satisfied in your own mind that you have found a worthy betting proposition. Pay all winnings straight back into the betting bank. As the bank expands, as hopefully it will, you will be able to gradually increase your stakes. But, for now, we are concerned solely with laying the foundations. This is an essential first step. Nobody can consider themselves to be betting professionally if they have not set aside a betting bank.

Hint 2: Open as many betting accounts as possible

Followers of the Pricewise and Sports Betting columns in the *Racing Post* will be more aware than most of the advantages of being able to secure early and fixed prices. No punter can afford to rule this type of betting out of his armoury, even if there are numerous frustrations attached to it, notably being 'knocked back'. Betting tax-free in the ring has many advantages, but there is no future in taking 4-1 or 5-1 tax-free when much bigger prices have been available in the off-course exchanges. In order to take maximum advantage of early-price betting, punters should avail themselves of as many credit accounts as possible, as well as having the necessary facilities for debit and switch card betting.

Now I appreciate that there are some who will not entirely trust themselves not to bet above their means if offered credit betting facilities. Two responses: firstly, only request a credit limit in line with your means and expectations; secondly, and perhaps more harshly, if you fear falling in too deep with credit betting, then you are advised not to take up the game seriously, because a punter who cannot trust himself in all situations is doomed to failure. One rider: do not bet using Switch or Delta, nor open credit (or worse) deposit accounts, with obscure firms without a long track record in credit betting or, preferably, a string of betting shops behind their operation. Or at the very least, do not expect to be paid if you hit a big win with these companies.

The sad rule of thumb is that any firm setting up to deal purely in credit and deposit betting is destined to fold. Some of these firms will take a sober and responsible view and cease trading after settling all outstanding debts. But many others will collapse owing money to unfortunate punters. The good name of bookmaking has been sullied by scores of these firms over the years, leaving creditors banging at the door. Therefore, all punters owe it to themselves not to bet with any firm that they cannot trust implicitly. As soon as a cheque is as much as a day late from any but the most long-established firms, bank it, hope it stands, and cease trading immediately.

Remember, gambling debts are not recoverable in law and there is no bonding system to protect punters from incompetent and unscrupulous operators, as in the City or the holiday business, for example. The law has never felt it necessary to give punters even the most basic of consumer protection. But this is no excuse for us not acting responsibly and we should undertake to settle our gambling debts promptly in return.

Hint 3: Set realistic profit targets

As already indicated, the targets you set should be related to the size of your betting bank. Let's assume your bank is £500. You plan to strike an average of four bets a week, with a stake of £25 each. At these figures, your annual turnover would be £5,200. You have aimed for a profit margin of 20 per cent - optimistic but by no means unattainable. Should you attain precisely this margin of profit, you will be £1,040 to the good at the end of the year. This of course makes no allowance for betting tax, or indeed out-of-pocket expenses such as form books, racecourse entrance, petrol and so on. Indeed, should all your business be done off-course, with tax paid on top of stake, your profit will immediately be sliced in half.

Those in Treasury departments and greedy bookmakers with an eye to underscoring profits by increasing the already punitive level of deductions should note that the effective rate of taxation on your bets will have been 50 per cent, a particularly burdensome impost by any standards - and, it should be noted, no great incentive to take up betting.

I always find an uneasy shudder passing through my system when I tot up the amount of tax I pay each year. In 1989 alone, the figure came to the best part of £12,000. If there is a more chastening indication of the perils of betting than effectively to write off such amounts before getting down to the business in hand, I have yet to come across it. The simple truth is that a punter betting purely off-course needs a profit margin of 10 per cent purely to break even. To think that great professionals like Alex Bird were happy with a rate of two per cent on turnover.

Sadly, the safest conclusion to make about off-course betting is that however well we do, the Treasury, the Levy Board and the bookmakers themselves will be doing a whole lot better. And all down to the seemingly innocuous deduction of 10 pence in the pound on all bets. Anybody out there still reckon this is an easy game to crack? Feel free to drop out now if the pace is too hot. Nobody would blame you. For the rest of us, it's back to the basics.

Hint 4: Establish a routine for form study

Only plan to bet on those days when you have sufficient time to properly study form. End immediately any bad habits such as scanning the newspaper in the lunch hour and having a couple of idle bets in the afternoon. The key point is to give yourself both time and breathing space in which to reach informed decisions. So often we are bounced into striking bets, especially on a heavily-tipped horse whose early morning price is likely to be quickly taken. Journalists may appear to have made out a good case, but if you have not done your own research you will be in no position to judge the value of theirs. Instead of waiting for the racing paper to drop on the mat in the morning, why not rise an hour or so early and take a brisk walk to the newsagent for it? Then make a pot of tea and take yourself into a quiet corner for some serious study. This applies especially to those living in busy households. You should have spotted the day's value before anybody else is up and about! I remember when I first left home to study in London. I made a rule that I would bet only on Fridays and Saturdays, when I was free of lectures, and would have just one nap selection on each of these days. I would leave my room early in the morning to buy the *Sporting Life* and would spend the entire morning working out my nap, which I would then back to level-stakes.

Looking back, this appears to have been an unduly rigid routine, but I have no doubt in my mind that adopting it was one of the best decisions I ever made. Not only did I spend the whole week looking forward to these two mornings, but I instigated a discipline which I would have been well advised to stick to in future, more prosperous years. It was as if those nap selections were carved from a rare stone, and that far more than the fiver or tenner I was staking depended upon them. I made sure I wrote down my reasoning in a special notebook. I used to spend the Friday afternoon studying in Senate House library. I would come out in mid-afternoon and pop my head around the door of the nearest betting shop to check on the result. It was the days of board markers, and my heart would be in my mouth as I scanned the neat lines of names - red for winners, blue for the placed horses, prices in black.

My nap was up there in red more often than not that first term. I would clench my fist in quiet triumph and take myself to a nearby cafe and celebrate with a pot of tea and an unfeasibly large cake, checking on tomorrow's runners in an edition of the *Evening Standard*.

Those days were vital in forging that essential requirement of any backer's make-up - confidence. I made all kind of resolutions in those days, not least to pursue a betting-related career in place of the stifling prospects offered by the law. Betting seemed to promise a rare and glorious sense of freedom - the freedom to forge my own destiny, to make decisions on my own behalf, for which I would be answerable only to myself.

This, at heart, is the appeal of betting, although the attractions are too often blurred by frustration and self-recrimination. Even allowing for the rosy hue of memory, I have no doubt that the early decision to follow a disciplined routine was one of the best I ever took, allowing me to feel purposeful and organised, like the professional I dreamed of becoming as I swelled with excitement in my seat in the cafe, wondering where my money would be going the following day.

Hint 5: Invest in form books

It would be marvellous to think there was a gilt-edged system which enabled us to spot winners after a quick scan of the runners in our daily papers. Naturally, there isn't, though there are usually one or two services being hawked around which promise as much. They are usually built around the form figures and logic a 10-year-old child would be quick to query.

Of course it is common sense to expect a horse with recent form figures of 111 or 321 to be preferred over one with 000, or even 234, but if betting was this easy the bookmakers would not have bothered inventing it. (Yes, I'm a conspiracy theorist on this one. Think about it. The first person to think of betting must have approached another with a proposition. Naturally, he would have believed he had an edge. And who usually has the edge in betting matters, but those gentle and magnanimous men the bookmakers. QED - as the say in the science journals.) In betting, all information must be placed into its proper context. Form figures of 111 do indeed look more promising than 000, until we discover the first horse has been running in sellers and the latter in Pattern races.

No punter can do without a form book, both for the current season and at least the previous two seasons, preferably more for National Hunt racing. It has to be admitted that prices of many services appear prohibitive, but try spreading the cost out over a season. For the frugal, there is the alternative of binding together the weekly results pull-outs from either the *Weekender* or *Raceform Update*. Although the two trade papers provide detailed form on a daily basis, it is simply not comprehensive enough to satisfy a serious backer. Do not try to cut corners by relying on this service. I have used the *Superform Weekly* for many years, and I am becoming increasingly impressed by the *Timeform Perspective*.

Both services give detailed finishing positions and distances on all races run in Britain and the leading foreign events, plus starting-prices, handicap marks and a time analysis. Superform scores in its summaries of a horse's past career (for instance "effective on firm and soft, stays 1m 2f, suited by a sharp track"), Timeform in its comprehensive race-by-race summary with hints about horses unlucky in running or likely to improve.

It is also essential to have access to a form, and ideally time, ratings service. The *Superform Weekly* and *Timeform Perspective* service come equipped with ratings, though subscribers to the former will have to take a little more time to sort them out, as they are not conveniently listed on a race-by-race basis. John Whitley's excellent *Computer Racing Form* is another product to consider. Alternatively, there are solid services provided in the *Racing Post* and *Sporting Life*. Ratings should be a treated as a rough overview, giving a quick, initial indication of the ability of each horse in a race before you commence your own more detailed analysis. Under no circumstances should ratings be followed blindly.

Summary

We have put aside a betting bank, of sufficient size and depth to enable us to plan ahead on a medium to long-term basis. The very act of creating the bank has given us a welcome sense of making a fresh start. We have opened a number of credit accounts with reputable firms and are ready to take advantage of switch card betting. We have set sensible targets and considered the implications of betting tax and expenses. We realise we need a regular routine for form study and have invested in a form book and a ratings service.

stage **two**

making selections

Hint 6: Watch your mood

This is a hint which applies at every stage of the betting process - and it is worth emphasising at the outset. We can all remember the day when we were down, frustrated or simply bored. Maybe the boss had been on our backs at work, or the bureaucrats had come up with another nonsensical scheme to improve "accountability and effectiveness", which had done nothing more than create extra paperwork and kept us in the office deep into the night. Or maybe relations were strained at home, or a heftier-than-expected bill had just landed on the mat. To tell the truth, we were feeling a little sorry for ourselves. We had tried to blow away the cobwebs in the pub the previous evening and were now feeling the effects, the day's racing cards seeming to tumble and blur before our eyes as we tried to focus on them in the morning paper.

A winner, we thought, that should do it. Just one good winner to sweep away the tension, to get us back on good terms with ourselves, to blast ourselves back into profit with Ladbrokes, Corals or Hills. Preferably Ladbrokes. Maybe all three in one hit. You never know. We had overslept for an hour, so there was not as much time as usual to study form. Pricewise was tipping a likely one in his column. There was no time to research the form and it looked a touch dodgy, but so be it. You have to be quick to get on these days.

Just after we had connected with our bookmaker and had the price confirmed, we realised we had not planned exactly how much to stake. Fifty pounds maybe, making a bet of £450-50. Maybe £60, to back it to win just over a monkey, a nice round figure. That should do it. A nice round figure.

"One hundred to win at the price, please."

"One moment please, sir."

Usually they knock you back. For once you wish they would. As soon as you called for that hundred you knew you were overdoing it. You are not even sure the horse is proven over the trip.

"That will be fine, sir. A bet of £100 to win on Elementary Mistake at 9-1. Tax paid?"

"Yes, please."

"That will be £110. Thank you for calling."

You put down the telephone. Outside, the dark clouds are banking in the west. Indeed, it is just starting to rain. In just over five hours time Elementary Mistake will be running at a racecourse not more than five miles from where you live, as the crow flies. It needs firm ground. The puddles on the road outside indicate it has been raining on and off all night.

There is a horse in the same race who enjoys some cut. One firm is out of line in showing 12-1. You scan its form. Two career wins out of 24, but one over course and distance on soft ground. You sense the price will soon be disappearing. The arm-waving ranter on *The Morning Line* has just put in a word for it. Derek has been outside in his wellies to confirm the state of the ground. In between the picture puzzle, turf trivia and a couple of schoolboy howlers of a sexual nature, he tells us the ground will be riding good-to-soft. Jim McGrath laughs raucously in the background. The day's guest wonders what on earth he or she is doing there. "It's entirely possible," ventures Oaksey.

Meanwhile, you are back on the telephone, placing a saver on this new selection. Actually not so much a saver, more another decent win bet - £1,000-80. It is not often you remember to ask for the fractions. And they lay it. You also have a saver on a third horse, one you recall getting you out of trouble one bleak afternoon at Kempton Park. It is certainly on the downgrade now - but, if successful, the tenner you have placed at 20-1 will recover your stakes on the other two bets.

You now settle down to study form, notwithstanding the fact that you have already staked close to your daily maximum allowance. You check up the winning form of your second bet, the soft ground specialist. A grand would come in handy - really handy. It had won a four-horse race by half a length from an outsider ridden by an apprentice. The favourite in the race had finished distressed. You snap the form book shut. McCririck is reviewing the papers on

The Morning Line. You turn down the sound. Twenty minutes and two aspirins later, a horse has caught your eye in another race. This time you closely investigate its chance and that of the other runners. It holds up. You check it again and begin to feel a tingle of excitement. This could be the one.

You make a rough assessment of the horse's chance. Say around 5-1. The big bookmakers are showing 7-1 and better on their text pages. An urge sweeps over you to strike a bet, a decent bet - then you remember your earlier wagers. None of them can compare with this horse - but there is nothing you can do about that now. You curse yourself. If only you'd waited, had more patience. What to do? Your mind is a whirlwind again. Forget the other bets, pretend they didn't exist, and have the sort of bet you would have had if you were starting with a clean sheet on the day? If only you could. But nobody thinks like that, do they? One bet affects the next and that the next, and a kind of spiral develops. It is as if you are not quite in control.

A sick feeling in the pit of your stomach tells you those earlier bets are doomed. What were you playing at? Perhaps it is one of those days when you should forget betting, forget this new proposition. Your judgment is probably off-beam in any event. You make another pot of tea, the third of the morning, and try to read the morning papers. It won't go away. Visions of your 5-1 shot cantering home play before your eyes. You can't let it go. But nor can you bring yourself to have a good bet, a proper bet. You're in too deep already.

You compromise. Sometimes your entire betting seems like a series of compromises. You ask for £50 at the 7-1, tell yourself it will probably be near that price at the off and you can top up then if necessary. Maybe one of the other bets will have come up and put you well in front and you can really go to town. But you should be going to town now. If you hadn't had those earlier bets, you could have taken a substantial interest on the other horse and felt relaxed, in charge. You'd have done the right thing. As it is...

It is raining outside, a long, slow, lazy drizzle, the kind of rain which creeps up on you and soaks to the skin. No fun in going racing today. You go back into the bedroom for a lie down.

◻ ◻ ◻

So there we have it. Not only do bad moods adversely affect your betting, they rob you of all enjoyment of it. They disorientate you and lead you to take decisions you would never have taken if you had been in charge of your faculties. Five minutes of careful self-examination could have prevented the above. Some days are just not good for betting and we must learn to recognise when they are upon us and heed their message. As it is, our black mood will no doubt deepen after our two hasty early morning bets run stinkers, and the saver comes with a flashing late run from an impossible position to finish third. We'll be beyond caring then - and will probably back our later selection even though the price is only 9-2.

It will finish second, as we had known it would, and we will feel like head-butting the betting shop wall. Just as this feeling sweeps over us, the man on our right will tell us the winner of our race was a certainty, and that he's had the forecast up as well - and we'll feel like head-butting him, too. We'll back one last, get-out selection in a 15-runner handicap and it will never be sighted.

An exaggerated tale perhaps, but not too exaggerated. Most of us can probably recognise ourselves in there somewhere. But if bad moods can negatively affect betting - and they surely can - what about good moods? What affect do they have? Can they swing the spiral in a positive direction?

Perhaps the link is not so immediate and profound as that between bad moods and bad results. If it is one of the golden rules of betting that negative thoughts are almost always punished, positive ones are not so readily rewarded. However, we must endeavour to follow the advice in the next hint.

Hint 7: Make the most of the good days

Think about those days when you woke with a song in your heart, the sun was shining and you had made it to the newsagent before the paperboy had started out, before he had been given a chance to stop halfway through his round in order to read the latest revelations about sex and scandal in one of the tabloids. What about those mornings when you had finalised your nap of the day before the average punter had finished mixing his hangover cure in the kitchen? These are the best days to be betting, when you are in the right frame of mind.

On such mornings your head is clear. As a result, your judgment is more likely to be cool and refined. You will be in charge of events in a way that you were not in the earlier example. No careless, hasty selections on these mornings. No under- or over-staking on horses whose chance you have had neither the time nor the inclination to investigate properly. No hopeless get-out selections late in the day. No feelings of rage and bitterness should your horse lose, merely a quiet comment about the way of things to your neighbour before you leave the shop. Some days you will be rubbing your hands with glee at the prospect of backing a selection. The more you think about it, the more confident and the more excited you will become. In my experience these horses inevitably run well and, win or lose, leave you infused with a feeling of satisfaction and full of confidence for the future. It is my guess that we all feel happier, more 'at home', betting at certain times of the year, or at particular meetings or favourite racecourses. Equally, there are times of the year and particular meetings when things seldom go well. I have a particularly poor record at Royal Ascot, for instance - and, with one or two notable exceptions, June has often been a poor month for me.

July, on the other hand, is my favourite month in the betting calendar, not least because of Dick Hern's exceptional record at this time of year. The very act of turning over the calendar from one month to the next is often sufficient to infuse fresh confidence. I have attended the Newmarket July meeting in 10 of the last 11 years and only once failed to make a profit over the three days. A combination of the weather, the high class racing and the relaxed atmosphere at this most appealing of racecourses invariably puts me in the right frame of mind for betting - and I am sure such a positive mood has made a difference to my results over the years.

It is a common observation about gambling that you should play up your winnings when "in the vein". Like a snooker player who finds the balls running for him, so results can seem to swing favourably for the in-form backer. It will be taking us into the realm of the occult to suggest that positive frames of mind can affect results (although there have been experiments undertaken in the field of psychokinesis, which suggest this might be so), but all backers will appreciate how there is a world of difference between approaching a betting opportunity feeling charged and expectant and doing so feeling negative and tense.

Whilst certainly wishing to counsel against recklessness, a knock-on effect can develop. The positive, confident backer will be alert and ready to spot good betting opportunities. Equally, he will tend to avoid mistakes. (The last thing you want after backing a good winner is to spoil it with a stupid bet in the next.) I remember one memorable example of a positive knock-on effect, although I did not benefit from it personally, as I was working behind the counter in a Ladbrokes betting shop at the time.

It was a frosty Saturday afternoon in early January. Only the meeting at Sandown Park had survived the weather and this after a series of morning inspections. A tiny charge ran through the entire shop on receipt of the news -

the prospect of a tedious afternoon limited to a few greyhound races is as unwelcome to betting shop staff as it is to the punters. The first winner was a popular one with many of the shop's regulars, coming in at 5-4. Most played up their winnings on John Francome's Wing And A Prayer in the next and he scooted home - again at 5-4. Nothing spectacular, but two winners to put most punters in a confident frame of mind. There was a definite sense of purpose in the shop and a growing tension. The adrenalin was flowing and it promised to be one of those rare afternoons when everything went the punters' way.

Equally important was the lack of diversions. Thanks to the abandonments, punters could concentrate their minds on the one race meeting. Business was unusually brisk behind the counter after the first two races and I noticed how the stakes were rising on bets in the next. Tens and twenties instead of the usual fivers. And nearly all the punters in the shop had chosen to back the same horse in the third race, the popular Grand National winner West Tip, who duly won in a driving finish up the long Sandown hill.

These were the days before live television was permitted in the betting shops. All we had to rely on was the Extel commentary, coming crackling and vague from a tiny speaker in the corner of the shop. Almost every punter in the shop began urging home West Tip, cheering and pounding the floor at the positive vibes from the commentator, whose orders were to enliven a race finish, to prolong the tension, to extend it as much as possible, however mundane it might have been in reality.

"And it's West Tip, still leading, a length ahead, 50 yards to go and Canny Danny is renewing his challenge... West Tip from Canny Danny, West Tip from Canny Danny... West Tip holding Canny Danny." When the winner was announced the shop burst into spontaneous cheering. Backs were slapped. Mark, the settler, gave a weary groan and dispatched me to the underground safe to bring in a spare thousand or so. The punters were already at the pay-out counter, voices raised, hands twitching. "Just look at their bloody faces," whispered our cashier, Liz.

I counted out the new money. "Keep it coming," said one of the punters, "it's about time we had a result out of you bastards."

Most punters played up again on the favourite in the next. Those who seldom staked more than a fiver could be seen nervously ruffling through their wad of fivers and tenners, wondering whether to have £50 on, maybe even £100. The word in the shop was that the next one couldn't be beat. It was a certainty - better than West Tip.

The horse's name was Beat The Retreat. It grappled its way home in another tense, elongated finish, making all the running and hanging on to win at odds of 10-11. Forget the skinny price, it was a winner. Another bloody winner! Just then, at that moment, the punters were free to feel the Ladbrokes empire tottering. And they could gauge it too, a tiny part of it, from the obvious pressure we were under behind the counter. The entire shop formed a chaotic line at the pay-out desk, goading and cheering as the winnings were counted out and hustled under the counter. Perhaps this was the day's peak.

The next race was a more complicated one, with no obvious selection to unite behind. At least five horses were strongly backed and many punters did find the winner, Cool Gin, at odds of 9-2. Those who had played up their winnings, yet again found themselves collecting fifties and hundreds instead of their usual pounds and pence. The final winner was also well backed. We had just enough money in the shop to settle all the bets. Had the favourite gone in, we would have had to turn away punters unpaid - the one thing, above all, that betting shop bosses dread. A week or so later, of course, most of the punters had given back their winnings and returned to their usual stakes. But the memory remains one of the few highlights from a tedious year I spent in the employ of Britain's most ruthless bookmakers.

A few weeks later, I was working in the marketing department at head office and was passed the nationwide returns on that week. There was a minus figure in the final column. Thanks largely to that one Saturday afternoon, the entire Ladbrokes betting operation had lost money on the week, an unprecedented and potentially calamitous matter for a public company. The marketing budget was slashed as the top floor panicked at the implications, leaving me largely free to read the *Sporting Life* and dream of my own fantastic winning sequence, as well as to formulate the idea which would later burgeon into the Pricewise column in the *Racing Post*. Within a year, Ladbrokes may have made me redundant, but I learned a good deal from my time at Harrow-on-the-Hill, not least how fragile is the bookmakers' position, if only we made up our minds to exploit it.

Hint 8: Beware the self-fulfilling prophecy

It is a sad commentary on betting that for every positive knock-on effect, there are a hundred negative ones. Many punters are almost permanently locked into a vicious spiral of losses, recriminations and yet more losses. A winner seldom does more than provide some temporary relief. If in doubt just look at the faces in your local betting shop. That Saturday at Ladbrokes was all too rare. Defeat tends to show on most punters' faces even before they have played. In betting, negative thoughts feed on each other like a virus. If you expect to lose, then so you will. If you are half-expecting a horse to blunder, or fall, or meet trouble in running, then so it will.

It is easy to try to blame events upon outside forces. "Would you bloody believe it?" comes the cry from a losing punter as his each-way selection weakens in the final furlong and narrowly misses the frame. Consider the last time you cursed fate and sent your crumpled betting slip hurtling across the floor. The chances are you had every reason to believe what had happened, for you had probably spotted the flaw in your selection before it ran. Maybe you had a doubt about the trip, the ground, or the form of the trainer.

A good example from my betting last summer concerns a horse called Moon Spin. Encouraged by the horse's recent form (she was on a hat-trick after wins at Chepstow and Redcar) and by Dick Hern's record at the particular meeting, I took a decent interest at the morning 12-1. The bet was by no means my worst wager of the year (I had correctly predicted the starting-price would be around the 8-1 mark) but there was a nagging doubt in my mind about her stall position. Moon Spin was drawn 1 in a field of 19 over on the far rails. Although she was a filly who tended to take a handy position, there was still a possibility she could be boxed in and fail to get a run.

However much I tried to convince myself the bet was a good one, and however difficult it might be for me to resist a horse of Dick Hern's, I could not get the doubts out of my mind. In the race itself, Moon Spin got off to a slow start and was repeatedly checked in her run as she attempted to extricate herself from the rails. Jockey Paul Eddery accepted the situation in the final furlong and allowed her to coast home. I remember cursing my luck as I came down from the stands - and again when she sauntered in next time. With a clear run she should just about have won the Newmarket race. I had been the victim of a self-fulfilling prophecy. I had told myself that in all likelihood Moon Spin would get trapped on the rails and get no sort of run and that is exactly what had happened.

Poker's 'Mad Genius', Mike Caro, believes it is the hand of the God of Irony, who is behind stories like the above - and many more of the agonising near-misses which are the stuff of our betting life. The God of Irony makes prophecies self-fulfilling. If, for instance, you are standing before the screen in a betting shop thinking, "Wouldn't it be just my luck if the jockey holds this horse up for too long and fails to get a clear run?" - then it is an unhealthy shade of odds-on that the God of Irony will intercept your idea and decide to use it. Do not give him this chance. If there are any doubts in your mind about a horse's chance, if you begin to find a picture developing in your mind of a calamity which may befall it, then leave the horse alone. You will seldom regret it.

Hint 9: Develop an appropriate betting style

The leading bridge expert Zia Mahmood once made the following observation about his style of play: "I live for the romantic moment, to tell someone I love them and then die. I play bridge for that, for one second of bridge beauty... I want to be outrageous and have a moment that's pure perfection." Each of us has a different approach to betting, a different style of betting.

Not everybody will favour Mahmood's cavalier approach, although it strikes a chord for me when I recall Nashwan's momentous wins in the 1989 2,000 Guineas and Derby. Some like to back the sure-things, short-priced favourites they cannot foresee being beaten. Others prefer the more adventurous style, backing the canny long-shot who can catapult them into profit at a stroke. Some bet win only, others each-way. Some choose exotic multiple bets. Some limit themselves to the top races, the championship events and big handicaps. Others like to root around for selling race coups. Information attracts many, others prefer to stick to their own opinions. The point is to develop a style which is appropriate for you.

Think of those selections and bets which have given you most pleasure (and try not to be too heavily swayed by the result). Was it the canny each-way shot who sneaked into the first four in a 16-runner handicap at odds of 40-1? The ante-post selection about whom you took 33-1 and who started 4-1 second-favourite on the day? Or the 4-5 chance who you assessed at 1-8, and who cantered up by a distance? Ask yourself: do I feel at home striking this or that type of bet? Some people would feel all at sea if asked to bet in a 16-runner handicap, feeling they could not possibly get to grips with all the complications. Others will relish the difficulties. Which bets do you place with confidence, and which trouble you?

I have never been happy with forecasts, although I appreciate there are times when such bets can offer excellent value. No doubt one reason would be my lack of success with such bets, but I also find it exceptionally difficult to arrive at a satisfactory assessment of odds and chances in such situations. I enjoy ante-post betting, and have found it profitable, but no doubt others find it too risky and speculative a form of betting. I can relish sorting out a Placepot on a day's card - others may feel they cannot see the wood for the trees when attempting such bets. Apart from always seeking value, there are no rules for preferring one betting style over another, other than to identify the one which most appeals to you and to develop it over time. The pleasure you gain from your betting is sure to multiply as a result.

Hint 10: Narrow down the races you plan to study

A related hint to the one above. Open a racing paper and you will be faced with a plethora of betting opportunities. This applies especially on Saturdays, but even on seemingly low-key Mondays there are often four meetings, plus greyhounds and sporting events. This book will concentrate on horse race betting, though much of the advice applies across the board, from Royal Ascot to rummy with the family on a wet Sunday. No serious punter will be expecting to bet every day, let alone in every race, yet neither do we wish for betting opportunities to slip through the net.

We need to establish techniques for spotting races which are promising for betting - and for rooting out those which are bookmakers' benefits. Much will depend upon personal preference, such as jump racing ahead of the Flat, but a good deal will also revolve around your character. Ask yourself: what approach do I take to my selection of possible races for betting?

If your best answer is, "Well, as far as I can see, none at all of note", then you have some work to do. Nobody can succeed at betting with such a haphazard approach. We have to satisfy ourselves that at the end of a session of study we have highlighted the best possible betting opportunities within our mode of operation. More often than not, of course, this will mean 'no bet today'. Think about some of the best bets you have struck. Then some of the worst. Are there any patterns to be detected? My guess is that a good many fascinating trends will develop if you take sufficient time over this process.

For instance, if you are something of a perfectionist, one who likes to bet only on nine-carat gold selections, it is a sensible assumption that your best bets have come in the top events, such as Group 1 races on the Flat and championship races over jumps. Here the form is reliable and the horses are more likely to give their running. You will no doubt prefer to take a short price about a proven performer than a bigger one about a more chancy proposition in a lower grade.

Indeed, your worst bets will probably have been when you dabbled in a handicap, just for fun, after a good win in one of your favoured events.

Alternatively, if you are one who enjoys solving puzzles and coming up with canny selections at tempting prices, you will probably prefer betting in handicaps. Sellers will appeal to those who relish the 'ducking and diving' side of racing and like to spot a horse who has been laid out for a touch.

Professionals such as Patrick Veitch of 'The Professional' fame like to concentrate on maiden events, trusting that the inside information they have received about unraced two-year-olds, in particular, will have put them ahead of the game. It all comes down to our professional's view about feeling 'at home'.

First scan the day's meetings. Are you more taken by the prospect of betting on races at Ascot, Carlisle or Market Rasen? When you have chosen your meeting, which of the races there appeals most tempting. The handicaps? The maiden events? Novice chases? Stop when you feel a tingle of expectation about a race. Maybe a favourite trainer has a runner. Or there is a horse in the field you noted as one to follow earlier in the season. These will be the races which will repay study.

Hint 11: Stick to your own opinions

For everybody who relishes a bet in a sprint handicap, there are three or four others who shy away in horror. The same for sellers, minor handicaps at jump meetings, and so on. People will often try to convince you that you are wrong to favour a particular type of race or horse. Authors of betting books are often the worst offenders, with their exhortations to "Never bet in handicaps", and so on. Ignore such nonsense. While there are statements which contain germs of common sense, such as "Beware of three-year-old handicaps in the first three months of the season", nothing is cast in stone.

All rules are there to be broken. This might appear to be a charter for chaos and confusion - and indeed it is for many punters who find it difficult to make up their minds. But we cannot afford to shelter behind rules which give the impression of solidity but are actually built on sand.

The only person who should be telling you where to bet is yourself. Take guidance, of course, and reflect at length upon it - but make sure you stick to your guns. There are far too many people in our everyday lives telling us what to do and what is expected of us without letting petty rules and restrictions tie us down in our betting as well.

Hint 12: Expect to take at least an hour studying a race

Would that there was, but there is no substitute for hard work in betting - at least for those who hope to make it pay. The more experienced you get, the easier it is to find your way around a card or race. But there is no escaping the sweat and toil. There have been times when I have been foolish enough to believe I could use my instinct to make selections after a quick scan of the morning papers, but I have always come a cropper. It is the first home truth of betting that you get only what you deserve. The gambling gods have many qualities, but sympathy has never been one of them. So when you have settled on your favoured races, it is time to get out the pen and paper. My rule of thumb is to be prepared to spend at least an hour over each race and quite possibly more in big fields.

Failure to do my homework cost me a good winner at the start of the 1993 Flat season, one which could have got my betting off to the best possible start. It was the first day of the Newmarket Craven Meeting. I was interested in a horse called Splice for the 3.05, the Abernant Stakes. I had undertaken a cursory study of the race and noted Splice's claims, but for one reason and another had not completed a full analysis. I had also resolved not to bet unless such rigorous analysis had taken place. Splice was sweating in the paddock, which deterred me further. (Detailed study would have revealed she is prone to do so and that it does not hinder her chance.) When I got to the ring she was showing at 10-1. I was deeply tempted, but had undertaken no value analysis, so was unable to do anything other than guess what would be the appropriate sum to have on.

I began toying with various figures in my mind (£1,500-£150? £2,000-£200?) and suggested to a friend that we watch the runners go down. Splice seemed in good shape. When I returned to the betting ring her price was down to 7-1. I retired to the stands to watch the race without a bet. As you will have guessed, Splice won - and did so comfortably.

Hint 13: Analyse every horse in a race

One of the commonest habits among backers is to develop a fancy for a horse, make a spurious case for it with a quick scan of the form and rush to back it before everybody else latches on. When it wins, we congratulate ourselves for being a superb judge and reach for the newspaper to check on the runners for the next race in order to repeat the dose. Getting into habits like these is not only injurious to successful betting, it is fatal. Fortunately the habit is easy to recognise, if not to break. But even the most disciplined among us need to be aware of another, related habit which can seep, unobserved, into our daily routine.

We will often commence studying a race when we have a fancy for a horse. Perhaps we will give ourselves a pat on the back for virtuously doing our homework instead of rushing to the telephone or betting shop. However, unless we are careful we might as well have had a blind bet, because there is a danger any study of the race will be coloured, if not tainted, by our original fancy for this horse. Here is an excerpt from my 1993 betting diary, on this very point. It was the day after Splice, so you will realise I was not in the best of form at the time.

Wednesday 14 April: 11.30am.

One horse caught my eye for today's racing - Beware Of Agents in the 2.35, a seven-furlong handicap. Having studied the race, I discovered there were too many doubts to be raised about his chance and decided I must leave him alone. The horse had not shown his form for some time and the stable was not in the best of form. An hour or so later, sitting in a Ladbrokes betting shop in the centre of Cambridge, I notice that a horse called Sovereign Page is attractively priced at 20-1 in the morning lists. He has a sound chance on time and form in a race which will not take a great deal of winning. I imagine he would be around 12-1 on my figures.

The problems are that he is without a run this season and once wore blinkers, suggesting he is not the most trustworthy of customers. I forget my earlier conclusions about not backing horses about whom I have doubts - and place a bet of £75 to win at the 20-1. I know as I place the bet it is a thoroughly lazy one - but I tell myself it would not be the first time this sort of horse has won for me. I leave the betting shop feeling strangely on edge.

Usually I get a holiday feeling when I check into a hotel for a race meeting - but yesterday evening I felt tense, even uneasy, as if I did not belong there. I know I am completely out of touch. A fluke 20-1 winner could be just the ticket to turn things around. I walk on to the station, summing up my thoughts. It is another grey, rather cold, depressing morning.

Evening: 9.30 pm

Confession time. I bet like a beginner this afternoon, a proper mug. I would not believe the following had happened if I had not done the same a hundred times before. When will I learn? A horse called Little Bean was all the rage in the 2.35, Beware Of Agents' race. The horse was down as needing a longer trip in my book, yet was offered at only 11-10. There was a huge tip for Little Bean on the racecourse (his trainer Geoff Wragg's horses often seem to attract heavy support) but I ignored that. He was now terrible value. Beware Of Agents was showing at a tempting 6-1. I told myself that however well he might have run in the Lincoln, he was not certain to reverse the form with another of the runners, Will Of Steel. And like Rutland Water, my bet yesterday, his best form came some time ago.

I thought about all these things, then found myself calling for £100 at the 6-1. I had broken not only this morning's resolution, but also my opening one of backing horses to win a minimum of £1,500. I was immediately disgusted with myself. I shamefully hid the offending ticket away in my inside jacket pocket. It was no use citing boredom as an excuse, or a need for a little action. I had acted like a mug.

I climbed to the top of the steps in time to hear Channel 4's Jim McGrath telling the world that Beware Of Agents had had a breathing problem. Skilled backers know these things before they bet. I had not. Beware Of Agents ran a moderate fifth of the six runners. The race was won by Will Of Steel, who comes from a stable I sometimes follow, and who was actually better value on my figures than Beware Of Agents, having been returned at 13-2.

At the time, I found my actions utterly incomprehensible, as if they had been the product of some force beyond my control. I had struck a bet I had no business making. The rest of the day was spoiled by feelings of bitterness and self-recrimination. Later, relaxed by a long walk, and sipping a pint of IPA in a riverside pub, I decided I had committed an elementary mistake, nothing worse.

Some time last season I had marked down Beware Of Agents as the type to win a decent handicap. He was, after all, a course winner at Newmarket off a higher, if perhaps flattering, handicap mark. As my eye had travelled down the list of runners in the evening paper, it had focused upon the one name - Beware Of Agents. I immediately allowed myself to believe I was onto something, and did not complete a proper and thorough appraisal of the field. Indeed, all subsequent analysis was built around the conviction that Beware Of Agents was the one for the race. I had been too hasty in dismissing the other runners.

It was not hard to believe that Gilt Throne and Little Bean were running over the wrong trip, that Euro Festival would need the run, and that Herora was too inconsistent to be fancied. But I was too hasty in feeling that Will Of Steel was too high in the weights. The Ramsden team would not run a horse from 5lb out of the handicap unless they considered he had a strong chance. And he was the in-form horse in the race. In trying too hard to mould my thoughts to fit a pre-conceived idea I had not only allowed myself to overlook the obvious selection, but had also skimmed over Beware Of Agent's faults.

I was like a chess player who thinks for too long over one move, closing out the other options. Sometimes it can work for a backer, latching instinctively onto one horse - but you need to be in much better touch than I am at present. The fact that I had eventually come to my senses about Beware Of Agents, yet still backed him, we can put down to the age-old dread of missing a winner; 6-1 did look a good price, compared with what I had been expecting.

You have to act quickly in the betting ring and earlier, calmer appraisals can be lost in the heat of the action. I had missed altogether until too late that Will Of Steel was also a good price. But there was no excuse for backing either horse, certainly not with a 'compromise' bet like the one struck. I should have gone to the stands and toughed it out. A professional would have done. A professional would also not have backed Sovereign Page, who finished a distant eleventh of the 13 runners. So much for my earlier hunch.

The points raised above are so important they are worth underscoring with another hint.

Hint 14: Study each horse objectively and in fixed sequence

The fact that we have a fancy for a horse should lead us to be extra rigorous about investigating its chance. Often it is tempting to assume we know all about the horse and it is this over-confidence which may lead us to overlook the vital flaw which will later cost it the race. But before we commence such rigorous study, we should do our best to put the fancy to the back of our minds. My advice is to analyse each horse in turn, starting with the top weight or no.1 in a race. Of course this will sometimes be the original fancy, but no matter because we are about to study each horse objectively. We are trying to dissect its chance in the manner of a biologist in his laboratory.

It was only in 1993, when asked by the *Racing Post* to help out on the Spotlight desk, that it was finally driven home to me how important it is to analyse each runner in turn. It is an excellent discipline having to explain your reasoning in public as a Spotlight writer. On the negative side, you do not want to overlook an obvious line of form, or discuss a series of outsiders without getting to grips with the leading fancies. The only way to avoid this is to take time checking out each runner. The bonus comes when you are proved right by tipping the winner - and hopefully by backing it, too.

Of course the other bonus is that you get paid for studying form! Backers working from home will not enjoy this luxury, but it is still sound advice at least to jot down your reasoning, if not write your own mock Spotlight. See if you can beat the journalists at their own game.

Hint 15: Check the key factors

Readers of *Value Betting* will be acquainted with my form and value system for assessing each runner. This involves attributing scores to each horse in the key areas of overall form, recent form, trainer, jockey, going, distance, track and, where necessary, draw. Backers who find such a procedure unduly complex or time-consuming should still compile a simple check-list of the vital factors.

Make sure you assess every horse for ground, distance, track and connections. Set out a box structure as indicated below. Tick the relevant box if you are satisfied the horse will be suited by the relevant conditions, and that its connections are in form and have shown themselves capable of winning a race of the type studied. Put a question mark if you are unsure and a cross if you believe the horse will be unsuited by the conditions, or if you have serious doubts about the connections. Examples here might be a stable without a winner for over a month or an inexperienced 7lb claimer against senior riders.

Horse	Going	Distance	Track	Connections
A	✔	✔	✔	✔
B	?	✔	✔	?
C	✔	✘	✔	✔
D	✔	✘	✘	✔
E	✘	?	?	✘

It is surprising how often this straightforward exercise will reveal a serious weakness in a horse's chance. The next move is to study your ratings service for a guide as to the relevant form chance of each horse in the race. Do not believe that because a horse is top-rated it must inevitably command most attention. Sometimes it will be possible to rule out certain horses because they are clearly outclassed.

But if our study is not to be coloured by our original fancy, neither should it be thrown off course by too slavish an attention to the top-rated horse in our service. Assessing a horse's chance at the weights is only one aspect of form study and not necessarily the most important. Ability to handle the ground will often be the more telling factor, especially when conditions are ranged at extremes. We need a greater degree of subtlety. Therefore, having compiled the check-list and noted the ratings, I suggest we consider the following question.

Hint 16: Ask yourself: what is the type of horse needed to win the race I am studying?

There will be as many answers to this question as there are races run, but posing the question is the best way to synthesise your horse-by-horse information. Look up the last five, or even 10 winners, of the race you are studying. This is often particularly rewarding in top events, but should not be underestimated in run-of-the-mill contests. Last Flat season, for instance, I discovered that three of the last six winners of a six-furlong handicap at Leicester had been won by trainer Paul Felgate.

His runner this time, Macs Maharanee, appeared to have an outstanding chance. I selected the horse and helped back it from a morning 7-1 down to 4-1 favourite. The horse was beaten a neck, but it was still one of those bets you can look back upon with total satisfaction. In big races, study of past winners can strongly suggest you should be following horses with proven Pattern race form against those stepping up from lower grades, or perhaps hint that you should prefer an improving three-year-old against established horses. A few minutes spent checking the history books will often help you narrow down your short-list of interesting horses.

Maybe, by now, you reluctantly feel your original fancy should be discarded. You double-check its form to make sure and find no reasons to change your mind. Be firm. We will all be able to remember galling incidents when we discarded our first choice and backed another, only to see the former hack up. In such situations, with confidence shaken, it is tempting to try to convince yourself you should rely on your original gut reactions instead of ploughing through the form.

Quite possibly, a know-all in the betting shop or racecourse bar will be on hand with a timely cliche, such as "never change your mind". You will probably nod lamely. Maybe next time you will strike a couple of bets after just a casual half-hour over the paper at breakfast. One goes in at a decent price and the other appears unlucky in running. You tell yourself you may have got the game licked at last and put the form books into a cupboard. Six months later you spot the same know-all propping up the same bar (these characters have the virtue of consistency, if nothing else) and you shuffle over to moan about the lengthy losing run you are enduring. Of course our know-all will have an opinion about how to put a stop to this as well and by now you are so desperate for a winner you feel there can be no harm in taking his advice, just for one race at least...

Betting is full of these tedious, if not vicious, circles and escaping them is half the battle. Try taking a few seconds out for reflection. Review the reasons for neglecting your original fancy. Maybe your thinking was faulty and you should have stuck to it after all. This will at least make you extra resolute not to make the same error next time. But chances are your reasoning was sound, even if the result has gone against you. Our know-all will blanch at this reasoning and will probably waste no time in telling us that, "It's the result that counts. An odds-on winner beats a 10-1 loser any day in my book." Perhaps he will pull a betting slip out of his pocket and point aggressively to a couple of winners he sorted out earlier in the day. Winnings from both will no doubt be running on to a gruesome favourite later on in the afternoon - but, no matter, our friend is sure he knows exactly what he is doing. Time for another hint here, even if it is diverting us from our current form-studying task in hand.

Hint 17: Think long-term

Almost anyone can be wise after the event. ('Almost anyone', because the definition of a mug is who one fails to learn even with the benefit of hindsight.) Our bore at the bar has probably made something of a career out of it. And almost anyone can appear wise before the event, providing they offer enough opinions on it. Our bore is world class in this department, too - and so are quite a few tipsters, those who recommend one horse to one client and another to the next. (Don't believe these characters exist only in *Minder*. A good many are running private and premium-rate tipping services right at this moment.)

We, of course, are cultivating a sense of detachment. It may not be sociable to ignore our bore at the bar in favour of a quiet five minutes reflecting on events, but so be it. Just because a horse you passed over has just hacked up, does not mean you should commence a review of your entire operation.

If you are doing the basics right - for instance not backing horses who are unproven on the ground or over the trip - the winners will come in time. Although I was bitterly disappointed that Macs Maharanee should have lost the Leicester race referred to earlier, I was able to come away convinced that if I kept backing similar horses I was certain to win in the long run. It should be every backer's aim to place only those bets which you can look back and reflect on with satisfaction - whatever the result.

Hint 18: Ask yourself: has the horse I am interested in shown itself capable of winning the type of race under study?

Back to our form study. We have completed our check list, noted our ratings and reflected on the type of horse needed to win the race under analysis. Let us assume we have a shortlist of some three or four horses still regarded as worthy of interest. Now to the above question. In order to minimise the guess-work it helps to be able to satisfy yourself that a horse has shown itself capable of winning the type of race you are studying.

Logically, this will usually involve ruling out maidens, which is no bad thing, especially in competitive handicaps, where they have an exceptionally poor record. Also to be ruled out will be those horses taking a steep rise in class, perhaps from a maiden to a Pattern race, or from a low grade handicap to a valuable one at an important track. Then there are those horses with winning form on a tight track now running on a galloping one (such as Catterick to York). Form often fails to work out properly in these instances.

If you have a big field, especially of sprint handicappers, it is almost essential to be following a horse who has proved itself under similar conditions. Some horses will give their form against a small number of rivals but are not so effective in the hurly-burly of a big field.

Then there is the question of handicap marks. If your horse has won races off identical or lower handicap marks, then it will be worthy of consideration. Equally, if a horse is running off its highest-ever handicap mark, perhaps after a good run of form, you will have to convince yourself it is open to enough improvement to deal with the rise.

Hint 19: Give preference to recent form

I have included this hint as much as a reminder to myself. Last season I found I was backing too many horses in the hope that they would return to form, without strong enough evidence to suggest they would do so. Once again, we are in the business of minimising the guesswork. I was often in a position of being able to answer "yes" to the question in Hint 18, but only on form established too long ago to be strongly relied upon.

Unless there are strong reasons to believe that a horse runs best fresh, always try to stick with those who have shown their well-being in the last six weeks. Macs Maharanee, for instance, although running four times unplaced, had shown enough in her previous race to suggest she was close to returning to form. If so, she was exceptionally well-handicapped, running off an 18lb lower mark than when winning at Yarmouth in 1990. Another of my bets from 1993 was Sapience in the Princess Of Wales Stakes at Newmarket's July Meeting. This horse had won this race in the past and had plenty of form in stronger Pattern races. But he had been below form in 1993 and had finished a moderate third of five on his previous outing just 18 days ago.

I told myself that Sapience would be better suited by the conditions at Newmarket and decided there was compensation in the morning price of 14-1 to offset my worries about his form. Yet even as I placed the bet, a voice in my head was re-stating the doubts, making me wonder if I was doing the best thing. If I had been brutally honest with myself - as all backers should be - I should have left the horse well alone. But at least after he was beaten, I was able to resolve not to get involved in this type of bet again.

Hint 20: Follow 'momentum' horses

These horses provide much stronger betting material than the Sapience-like selection and we should all be on the look out for them. A momentum horse is a fast-improving type, with recent winning form. The key point is the winning form. Beware horses with placed form, however impressive this form might appear. It is probably a fluke. It is a good idea to stick with 'winners' in any form of life and betting is no different.

Pay particular attention to momentum horses winning in a fast time (indeed pay attention to all horses winning in a fast time). In particular, look out for those horses who show an ability to quicken at the end of a race, settling matters within strides. It is particularly difficult for the handicapper to keep tabs on such performers. Handicaps are the ideal medium in which to support the momentum horse - but be prepared to follow these horses if raised in grade to Listed or Pattern race class. My all-time favourite trainer, Dick Hern, is a past master with the momentum horse, although the Major's career has appeared to be sadly in decline following his unforgivable expulsion from West Ilsley at the end of the 1990 season.

I still glow at the memory of Gold Seam in the 1989 season. Having shown promise on his first two starts, Gold Seam first came good in a minor race at Leicester, quickening in decisive style to win impressively and recording a fast time into the bargain. To the uninitiated, Gold Seam might have appeared badly handicapped on his next start, when carrying top weight in a race at Newmarket. Most rating services would have endorsed this view - I recall him being bottom of the famous and much-trusted Timeform ratings. But as we have learned - and as Timeform themselves acknowledge - ratings, in themselves, are utterly inadequate for making selection. You have to read between the lines, in particular to look out for those horses you strongly believe are capable of stepping up on their form so far.

Gold Seam was one such example. I believed, to a point of certainty, that he was a genuine odds-on shot in the Newmarket race and wagered accordingly at the early prices, averaging just under 3-1 for my money. He cantered in at 9-4. Hern chose a Pattern race for his next assignment, the Kiveton Park Stakes at the Doncaster St Leger Meeting.

To the uninitiated, he would have again appeared to have plenty on his plate on this occasion, especially as he was opposed by the 2,000 Guineas fourth, Markofdistinction. Close followers of the horse, and of the Hern yard, would have had no such qualms. This was a race the Major had won four years ago with a similar sort in Lucky Ring, a momentum horse who was on a roll following a brace of wins in top handicap company. In comparison to Gold Seam, Markofdistinction, though boasting the stronger form on paper, had been plagued by a number of minor niggles throughout the season and had been relatively lightly-raced.

Again, it was necessary to read between the lines to get to the value. It was one of those marvellous days in betting when you identify a horse who you know will win, barring accidents. It was possible to obtain ample 7-2 in the morning lists. Gold Seam won impressively at odds of 9-4. I even had him in a substantial double with an earlier 6-1 winner. Oh, happy days.

Hint 21: Choose a stable to follow

This hint follows inevitably from the above discussion. It was the best decision I have ever made in betting to decide to follow the Dick Hern stable early in the 1980s. Nearly all my most memorable coups (and heart-stopping near misses) have come on horses trained by the Major, including Sun Princess, Merce Cunningham (five wins on the bounce in 1988), Minster Son, Nashwan, and scores of lesser-known two-year-olds and handicappers. Get to know a trainer's methods. With which type of horse has he or she enjoyed best results? At which courses, or meetings, does the yard have a good record? Which are the notable jockey bookings? Does the stable tend to hit form at a certain time of the year? In advance of a season, study a list of the trainer's horses. Assess their likely potential. Make your own plans. Which would be your Guineas horse? Which looks a live type to lay out for one of the big handicaps? Unlike others I could name, I have stayed loyal to the Major in the last three seasons, and have managed to make a profit backing his runners, despite his relatively poor record since leaving West Ilsley.

If searching afresh for a stable to follow, I would choose from between John Gosden, Michael Stoute, Roger Charlton and Henry Cecil, with preference for the last-two named. Cecil's record over the last decade has been one of supreme consistency and anybody paying close attention to his runners in that time must surely have finished on the right side. Mary Reveley and Oliver Sherwood are my two top jumping names. Please do not feel a need to limit yourself to the above trainers but do make sure your yard boasts a win-to-run ratio of at least 15 per cent and preferably nearer 20 per cent, judged on at least the last three, and ideally, five seasons' results. These stables should also have a relatively consistent record, year-on-year. Cecil would again be the paradigm example in this regard.

Hint 22: Follow stables in form and beware those out of form

No prizes for originality over this hint, but one which bears emphasising. Success breeds success and when a stable is in peak form its runners have a habit of performing above themselves. Often this spell will last for no more than a fortnight, but three or four timely winners from within this period might make all the difference to a season's betting. Equally, we must be beware of stables which are out of form. Of the two, this is perhaps the more pertinent hint. It is not just the virus and other similar disorders which can affect performance, there are also times when stables are simply not firing. Just as success breeds success, I am afraid that failure breeds uncertainty, frustration and more failure. (This is something we, as punters, will know only too well from our betting.)

I am sure this feeling of anxiety and frustration communicates itself to the horses, perhaps through the reins of a worried jockey who is being blamed for recent failures and fears for his position. More bad results follow and so the cycle continues. We, as punters, can stand aloof. Check the trainers-in-form figures in the *Racing Post* and, better still, keep your own charts for your favourite stables.

If a stable's win-to-run ratio is running at a rate of 20 per cent less than the average over a space of 10 or more days - BEWARE! Equally, if it is running at a rate 20 per cent or more higher than the average, now is the time to consider striking some thick bets. One more hint concerning trainers...

Hint 23: Pay close attention to a stable's second string

Such horses can often represent excellent value. Just because a stable jockey has preferred one horse to another does not give the punter licence to dismiss the other contender. The jockey might have agonised for hours over his decision and, like us, they are capable of making mistakes. Do think hard about these hints on trainers. They are among the strongest and most important in the book.

Hint 24: Don't knock sprint handicaps

I used to be one who groaned inwardly when faced with the prospect of a big field of sprint handicappers. So often they seemed to take turns beating each other and it was not always easy to gauge the effect of the draw. And one slip, such as a slow start, usually cost dear. Now, thanks in no small part to the encouragements of the *Racing Post*'s own sprint handicap expert, Emily Weber, I realise these races can offer tremendously exciting opportunities for the serious backer, particularly in the bigger events. I do not think it is any coincidence that my three best bets of 1993 were all sprinters. More of these bets later. For now, here is my betting diary for Saturday 31 July, when I backed How's Yer Father to win the Vodac Stewards' Cup.

Saturday 31 July: morning

Big Mac is in top form on The Morning Line today (you know, the sort of form which makes you wonder if the men in white coats are waiting outside the studio, needles primed.) He has ringed a long list of nap selections from his despised hacks and thrust them under the camera in his bejewelled hand. These gullible creatures have chosen to nap in the Vodac Stewards Cup this afternoon.

   Big Mac wants to know what on earth has possessed them to make their best bet of the day one from among 29 runners in a six-furlong handicap. A serious question, even if one is entitled to muse upon the qualifications McCririck has for judging the tipping of others. I feel obliged to answer it because my bet of the day, indeed one of my bets of the year, is in the self-same Stewards Cup. It's How's Yer Father.

Only the previous evening, I had toured the local betting shops discreetly helping myself to the 25-1. Credit accounts were also raided. The bet placed was £8,000-£320, with enough profit from the place element to pay the telephone bill and a handful of other demands languishing on my desk. May I recommend this relaxed method of placing your commissions. Not only does it avoid the stressful early morning scrum on the credit lines, but it also pre-empts the bookmakers from reforming the market should an early non-runner be announced.

Reforming the market, of course, being a euphemism for shortening horses without taking a bet and wriggling out of potential liabilities. This is the tactic many bookmakers adopted earlier in the week, following withdrawals from the Tote Gold Trophy and Leslie and Godwin Spitfire Handicaps.

Others, seeing it suited them better, chose to invoke Rule 4. Any steps we can take to protect ourselves from these sharp practices must be taken. Having asked a friend to secure a little of the morning 28-1, I have amassed what I choose to refer to as a 'hibernation bet', namely one which, should it oblige, will enable me to survive the winter as cosily as a tortoise in its box.

But back to Big Mac. Should I honestly be playing, let alone so heavily, in a 29-runner sprint? One in which, moreover, we are somewhat in the dark regarding the effects of the draw? My answer to this question, if posed generally, would have to be, "Most certainly not, unless you have exceptionally strong reasons for so doing." Well let me tell you, I have these strong reasons - reasons which are so strong as to leave me convinced that How's Yer Father is going to run a mighty big race this afternoon.

1) *I have studied the race in depth, having covered the meeting for Spotlight at the Racing Post. Of course it is impossible to cover all the angles in such a big field, but I have satisfied myself that I have looked into a good many of the most important.*

2) *The horse is in form, a vital matter in these big sprints.*

3) *He has proved himself in a big field. Again, vital.*

4) *He is well-handicapped, running off 4lb lower mark than when winning the valuable Ayr Silver Cup last season.*

5) *He is the Topspeed selection on this Ayr run.*

6) *He will appreciate any give in the ground.*

7) *Nearly all his best form is on switchback tracks.*

8) *And what we know about the draw suggests a position in stall 13 need not hinder his chance, even if a higher number might be preferable. (It is impossible to be without doubts about any selection, let alone a 25-1 shot in a big sprint handicap.)*

*I can make no equivalent case for any other horse in the race, though I do choose to have
a small saver on Arabellajill who looks value, too, at 16-1. The more I thought about
How's Yer Father, the more convinced I became that he simply had to go close. In fact I
spent so much time thinking about the horse I was in a hurry to complete my analysis of
the other races. I was also convinced that his starting-price would be a good deal shorter
than the morning 25-1, if not quite anticipating the gamble which would bring him in to
10-1 co-favourite.*

How's Yer Father finished a close third, running on well in the closing stages,
thus vindicating my judgment, if not providing the pay-day I had hoped. That
day will surely come. And I will not be at all surprised if it comes from a bet in
a sprint handicap.

Hint 25: Satisfy yourself that your selection will be trying

It is a sad comment on British racing that there is a need to include this hint.
Thanks to the current inflexible and petty whip guidelines, our stewards are
more intent on punishing riders for trying too hard than for not trying at all. If
you are betting in the top events there should be little delay in answering in the
affirmative.

But be wary of horses running in lower-grade contests, particularly small
handicaps. Is there any danger your selection might be 'having a run' to get its
handicap mark down for another day? If nothing else, asking yourself this
question will ensure you check on distance, going and track requirements. If
your selection is running over what appears to be an inadequate distance, or is
unproven on the ground, you probably should not be backing it whether it is
doing its best or not.

Hint 26: If in doubt, stay out

Often lengthy study of a race will have served to throw up nothing of interest.
Equally there may be three or four horses who look to have something of a
squeak but are impossible to separate. This is a danger point. Nobody likes
wasting their time and this is how it can feel if you have spent an hour over the
form books only to feel more confused at the end than when 'you started. The
temptation will be to pick out a 'just for fun' selection to back in order to give you
an interest in the race later on. Maybe you will revert to your original fancy, which

will probably still have a hold on your emotions despite having its limitations exposed by analysis. Have these fun bets by all means, but do not expect to look back on them with any kind of satisfaction at the end of the season.

Alternatively, you have a handful of possible selections and the strong suspicion that the winner is in there somewhere. The temptation here will be to take a stab in the dark and to favour one of the runners ahead of the rest. You will have no great reasons for choosing it, but then no great reasons not to either. And, again, it will only be for a fun bet, just to keep up your interest. Occasionally, your selection will win and leave you with a guilty sense of triumph, like a child stealing sweets from under a newsagent's nose. But more often than not, another from your original short-list will oblige, leaving you feeling bitter and frustrated, aware that you have wasted not only your time but your money as well.

Hint 27: Try to be fully confident about your selections and watch the doubts

A related hint, but one which bears examination. There are times when you back a horse despite not being fully confident about its chance. My suggestion is to leave these horses alone. Of course you can never eliminate every doubt from your mind - especially if, like me, you prefer to back relative outsiders, rather than favourites or second-favourites. The market can often play a part in inducing these bets. Perhaps you know, or sense, a horse will be strongly fancied, and will start at a much shorter price than that available in the morning lists. It is satisfying to beat the starting-price comprehensively (and a useful target to aim at) but only half the battle. One such example from my 1993 betting, again from the first April meeting at Newmarket, concerned a horse called Rutland Water.

On its best form, this horse was exceptionally well-handicapped. It represented the excellent Reg Akehurst/Richard Quinn combination. What is more, I was in possession of (almost certainly) reliable information that the horse was to be doing its best. With the Akehurst stable not averse to enjoying a gamble, I knew the morning 12-1 would not be lasting long and I estimated the starting-price would be around the 6-1 mark. (In fact the horse went off at 9-2, having touched 100-30 in the morning lists.) I took a decent bet at the morning 12-1, despite the fact that I was worried about the long gap since his last Flat run. Would he be sharp enough, despite the positive information? I had my doubts and was also worried about some less than sparkling recent outings over hurdles. There were excuses for these failures but they were disappointing nonetheless. My suspicion, subsequently confirmed, was that the horse would finish a one-paced third or fourth. He came fourth. Yes, I'd struck what appeared to be a marvellous value bet, but I was not fully confident about it and had suspected before the off that it would have been better to have stayed out.

Hint 28: Beware of 'inside information'

We are now approaching the end of our form study, and hopefully centering on a selection which we hope to be backing. The puzzle, it might seem, is close to being solved - in the manner of a crossword, perhaps, or maybe a mathematical equation. Yet is it? Tempting though it is to try to elevate form study to a pseudo-science, and much though the need to deal with figures might (almost certainly wrongly) deter the non-mathematically inclined from getting involved, form study is built on far shakier foundations than either of these disciplines.

However hard we work, when it comes down to it, we will have only opinion to show for our efforts. All we will be able to do is to make out a case for our selection, in the manner of a court room lawyer. Opinions are fragile things, easily swayed. Every punter will remember a time when they changed their mind from a seemingly confident selection after reading the views of a newspaper tipster, or perhaps after listening to a friend (or even a total stranger).

The professionally-minded punter has to learn to trust his opinions and to stick by them. There is no point in spending time studying form if we are to change our mind after the window cleaner knocks on the door to pass on a tip for another horse in a race. Too many punters, and newspaper tipsters, are obsessed by 'inside information'. They lack the confidence to stick to their guns and prefer to shelter behind the views of others. There is an alchemical quality to inside information - one word from an 'inside' source promises to turn base metal into gold.

Of course nearly all inside information is third-hand clap-trap, but this does not stop punters gravitating towards it like wasps around a jam pot. During the Newmarket July Meeting in 1991, some friends and I were discussing a race in the bar of our hotel. It was past midnight and the room was otherwise empty. After long study earlier in the evening, I had found a horse who I was rather keen on, but there appeared to be no great display of enthusiasm among the rest of the party. Somewhat miffed, I changed tack and suggested that should a drunken man fall down the stairs into the room we were occupying and convey to us a tip for the self-same race, we would discard my advice and heed his every word, as if he were some wizened guru possessed of an ageless wisdom.

Moments later, the door opened and in stepped a grey-haired man, dishevelled and clearly the worse for wear. He looked at the metal cage preventing access to the bar, and moaned about the licensing laws. Then he noticed the opened copies of the *Racing Post* on our table. He sat down with us and told us he'd got a tip for a horse running tomorrow. The only problem was, what with one drink and another, he could not remember the name of the beast, nor the race in which it was running. All he could recall was it began with an 'H' and there were two words to its name. One among our party began a frantic search through the declarations.

"What about Harvest Girl?"

"That's it," he burbled, "Harvest Girl. Don't miss out, alright?"

Minutes later, he was gone. I need not tell you, I imagine, that Harvest Girl won - and that she did so at what is commonly known as 'a working man's price'. My horse, long since forgotten by all but my lone self, mooched in about eighth of 10. Punters love inside information in the same way they are drawn towards 'a certainty' or 'a good thing'.

The language of betting is full of these expressions, each seeming to banish doubt from the mind. It is as if there is a secret solution to each race, possessed by those privileged enough to be in the know. Oh, to be in that number! This is not betting, it is a kind of bogus faith healing. The truth is that most punters are herd animals. Many follow markets moves, favourites and tips blind, as if such a strategy absolves them of responsibility for their failings. Equally, a rigid orthodoxy grips many newspaper tipsters. The most ridiculous notion I have heard for a long time is that of the 'professional' selection, the horse you should be tipping if you follow the correct procedures.

During the early days of Pricewise, I was once hauled over the coals by senior journalists for tipping a 40-1 shot in the Lincoln. The selection, it was said, had been pure guesswork. We needed more objective methods to underpin our selections. I bit my tongue and quietly pointed out that the horse may not have been the strongest of selections, but that tipping will always come down to guesswork - educated, inspired or otherwise - and there was no way I was changing my methods to fall in with the conventions of others. What is more, a 50-1 had just been named the winner of the Lincoln, one among a serious of big-priced shocks in the race. What I said in private at this outrageous and dangerous nonsense is not printable. (Nor, I imagine, is the response of my critics after I deliberately and provocatively selected the same horse in a race over a totally different trip next time.) I think a further hint is called for, to emphasise the above.

Hint 29: Don't follow the herd

There will be times when there appears to be an easy solution to a race - a horse who is clearly best on form, who handles the prevailing ground and is certain to stay. But the chances are that everybody else will have reached the same conclusion, not least our generous and enlightened friends, the bookmakers. We like to think of betting as a war between punter and bookmaker, but the truth is slightly more uncomfortable.

Betting is a largely a war between punter and punter. However much the PR merchants at the big bookmaking firms like to emphasis the former - with quotes about "taking on the punters" and figures (often plucked out of the sky) about liabilities bravely incurred - life is actually a good deal less interesting for our friends on the other side of the counter. In reality, they are nothing more than money managers, or 'turf accountants', as they used to call themselves in the days when betting shops had sawdust on the floor and were considered dens of vice and iniquity.

Perhaps this explains their humourless countenance, typified by BOLA's Mr Cheerful, Tom Kelly. The bookmaker has to win, otherwise he goes out of business. The punter, on the other hand, lives in hope - he is free to dream. After all, not many win at betting, indeed hardly any in the long run after the taxman has taken his share. It is a far from inconsequential achievement to end up on the right side of the profit line at the end of a year's betting. As a rough guide, 80 per cent of stakes are returned on bets struck off-course. Of the remaining 20 per cent, some 8.5 per cent goes to the Treasury, around one per cent to the Horserace Betting Levy Board and the rest is (gross) profit to the bookmakers.

Gross is used here as opposed to net, not as a comment upon the "leech-like role of bookmakers", to use trainer Luca Cumani's memorable, if not altogether fair description of them. After they have paid costs - largely wages, but also electricity, rent, rates, SIS fees and the many other niggardly charges which beset any business - the average bookmaker's net rate of profit is between two and three per cent. Now two or three per cent of Ladbrokes' or Hills' business is a very handsome sum indeed, equating to many millions of profit. (The bookmakers never discuss exactly how many millions, which is perhaps telling.) Yet two or three per cent is a margin of profitability which would be regarded as profoundly unsatisfactory at many another big company, Sainsburys or Tesco for example.

Occasionally Mr Kelly has a point, behind the grimace. I think we should dwell upon one pertinent matter here, and dwell on it for some little time.If we were all to improve our betting by as little as four or five per cent, the bookmakers would be broke. We'd have driven them out of business. They couldn't survive. It shouldn't be too difficult to achieve that extra four or five per cent. Adherence to a number of the hints in this book should help. Here is a check-list of extra suggestions, seemingly of minor importance, yet if acted upon, potentially lethal to the British bookmaking industry.

1)   Rarely, if ever, back Tricasts.
2)   Avoid through-the-card doubles on BAGS meetings.
3)   Every time you fancy a multiple bet, trade down one unit (e.g. if you fancy a Yankee, knock out the weakest of the four selections and have a Patent or Trixie instead. If you fancy a Patent, knock out the weakest selection and have two singles and a double instead. Shouldn't be difficult should it? Yes? Well think about the last time you did a Yankee. There was one selection in there, wasn't there, just to make up the numbers? A short-priced favourite, I don't doubt. Didn't it get beat? See what I mean?
4)   Never back odds-on in a betting shop.
5)   Stop popping into the betting shop to see how the results have gone and having a couple of little bets just to pass the time.

It should be easy. If we were to act on these essentially trivial hints we could win the war with the bookmakers, or at least share in their downfall. (Although improving by four or five per cent would leave an overwhelming number of punters still firmly in the red on their betting).

But remember the earlier point about the war between punter and punter? This comes first. The war between the punter you are and the punter you could be if only you started to get your act together.

It is a sad commentary on Britain's punters (and no doubt those in every other nation under the sun) that we bet and bet and bet - and hardly ever learn a single thing from our mistakes. We make life easy for the bookmakers. They just wait behind the counter to process the ill-considered rubbish we so often hand over on those innocent little slips, closely followed by our hard-earned cash. We know that 20 per cent of that hard-earned never comes back, yet what do we do about it on the whole? Nothing. The bookmakers may feed off weakness, laziness, tiredness and the many other bad habits which have taken us over. They may, at times, do so cynically and without humour. But we can't blame them. They are only doing their job. Our future lies entirely in our own hands. Isn't it time we began to make a move?

Hint 30: Make your mind up in advance about your selections

It would not surprise me if a majority of punters are in the habit of visiting the racecourse or betting shop with only the roughest idea of the horses they are interested in backing. They tell themselves they hope to get a feel for the day as it progresses. Of course it is important to note the going, and perhaps the well-being of the horses in the paddock if one is proficient in the field, but to be ill-prepared leaves one pray to idle gossip, and almost certainly to the type of panicky, ill-informed, last-minute selections which can help wreck a season's betting.

We, of course, will not be falling into such traps, so let us return to the apparent calm of our form study. We have, in our own good time, hopefully singled out a number of horses who we feel might repay an interest, horses who have survived our stringent analysis. Maybe a couple of these horses are beginning to get our pulse racing. Maybe we are now believing we may be on to something. Occasionally a horse will seem to jump off the page at you. This is one of the best feelings in betting. The more you look at the horse, the stronger it seems. You cannot wait to get involved. Here is one of the (sadly, rare) examples from my 1993 betting diary. It concerns Macs Maharanee, the selection mentioned in Hint 16.

Saturday 5 June: am

I've got one today. A horse I know is going to just about win. It's Macs Maharanee in the 7.45 at Leicester. The race is a six-furlong sprint handicap, Grade E, for horses rated 0-70. Macs Maharanee runs off 56. She is a six-year-old mare with a career record of three wins from 33 starts, who missed the whole of last season through injury. You can go very badly skint backing these horses, but there is a feeling in my water that Macs Maharanee is going to get me out of a whole lot of trouble this evening.

I was invited to do the Leicester Spotlight by the Racing Post yesterday. It is important when analysing such minor meetings to allow optimism to triumph over experience. You tell yourself, as you plough through so many bad sellers, claimers and 0-

70 handicaps, that the name of at least one horse is going to spring from the page at you and induce all those feelings of agitation and expectation, which are betting's unmatchable thrills.

Macs Maharanee had won sprint handicaps from marks in the mid-70s two years ago. She was steadily returning to form. Tomorrow's six furlongs on firm ground would be ideal. I felt a rush of nervous tension. What price would she be? How much would I want on? How much would I get on? What could go wrong? Emily Weber, whose ability to sniff out the winner of a complicated sprint is unparalleled within the walls of the Racing Post and quite probably anywhere else in this troubled land, whispered into my ear that the stable, that of Paul Felgate, had won tomorrow's race three times in the last six years.

There is only one thing left to do having assimilated such knowledge - and that it is to tell everybody of your discovery, one at a time. Soon, the entire office knew about Macs Maharanee. I have been away from the Racing Post for so long now that I have all but forgotten the essential driving force behind tipping and betting - the search for self-justification (and, you might argue, the ego trip which often accompanies it). The great joy of a Pricewise headline winner was precisely this - seeing its name in lights, and mine beneath it.

Forget the money. Since I have been away I have many times come back from a betting shop having backed a big winner, put the kettle on in an empty flat, congratulated myself for a job well done and moved on to something else. I tell you it is just not the same, backing them for yourself. (And I used to be paid a salary as well.) My minimum price for the horse is 6-1. William Hill, who release their early shows a good half hour before the opposition, are quoting this price.

I take a cautionary £100 to win. Ladbrokes, I soon discover, are going 7-1. I ask for £250 at the price. After a long delay, I am offered £50 at the 7-1. Insult is then added to injury as I am informed that I can have the rest at 5-1. First they take your information for a paltry consideration, then they try to get you to take under the odds for your selection. Ladbrokes will know perfectly well they can lay off any bet I strike at 5-1 at a bigger price. There is no time for - nor any point in - arguing. The big bookmakers have been getting away with these tricks for years.

I ring off, then put two contacts in to try to back the horse for me at the 7-1. One is knocked back to next to nothing, the other gets a hundred on at the price. Meanwhile, I am making a valiant assault on my record down to the local Ladbrokes. Three hundred yards in not much over a minute, despite having to elbow through a party of young children emerging from the Kentucky Fried Chicken. I pause outside the shop and take a couple of deep breaths. No, I confirm to myself, it is not that recurring nightmare I used *to have of rushing to a betting shop for such a big winner only to find that none of the pens work and that nobody will accept my money.*

I grab a betting slip and the first available regulation red pen. It has run dry. A cashier, noting my troubled countenance, sympathetically pushes another under the counter. There is enough in my wallet for £80 to win, but insufficient coins in my pocket to pay the tax. A call to head office confirms the price is still available. The bet is accepted. I fold the slip into the back pocket of my shorts. It is already upwards of 70 degrees and there are pools of sweat under the arms of my t-shirt. I buy a copy of the Sporting Life and read it in the shade in the park. Their Leicester Spotlight man has also napped Macs Maharanee. Like me, he has put it in at 7-1. But the starting-price, I am sure, will be nearer the 4-1 mark. No need to worry if this is a good bet, even if they have had me spinning around in circles to get on. (You do wonder, at times like this, whether it can all be worth it.)

Macs Maharanee was not due to run until early evening, leaving a long wait before my fate was known. The bet had excited me so much I made sure I recorded my thoughts.

The hours before a big bet can slip into a horrible void, like waiting for a lover to phone. When the time finally comes to walk to the betting shop to watch the horse run, I am sick with tension. My legs and upper arms ache and my mouth is dry. It is as if a series of tiny holes have been secretly punched into my system and are draining my strength away. And these are the feelings we pay good money for, time and again.

There are three punters in the betting shop - two forlorn regulars and a tall, professorial gentleman who appears to be making detailed calculations on the back of a betting slip. The screens inform me that Macs Maharanee has been backed down to 4-1, just as predicted. They are circulating at the start. I joke with the three figures behind the counter about the lack of trade. "I'm not staff," says one of the women, pointing to the manager. "It's just the only time I ever get to see him."

I sit in one of the hard-backed chairs, a couple of yards from the screen. Numerous flies are playing hide and seek in the air above me. The door has been left open to help with the heat and the commentator's words are emptying onto a disinterested street. They are under orders, and off - and the pins and needles mass in one of my arms. Had there been a drink to my side, or a cigarette in my hands, I would have automatically reached for it.

The horse is held up, going well. No missed break, no early barging. After two furlongs, I relax, safe in the knowledge that she will be involved in the finish. This feeling of calm - of inner peace even - could sum up the joy of betting, if ever there was any time to dwell on it. *Turmoil always returns. The jockey takes a couple of positions, switching to the inside over a furlong out. For an endless, slow-motion second it seems he will not - cannot - find room on the rails. The pressure builds inside me, close to bursting point - and then she is free.*

A length clear, sprinting home. I start to celebrate inside, awaiting the sweeping surge of freedom which accompanies such a winner. So many yards out - was it 50? - I scanned the remainder of the field. One horse was making a challenge. The commentator, it seemed, was urging it home. I searched for the post, for the winning line, but it did not come in time. The other horse, whose name was Blue Topaze, got up close home. I knew it had, even though the angle was poor. The judge called for a photograph - but I was resigned already, immersed in a familiar, hopeless rage.

I left the betting shop and scanned the cloudless sky and the tangerine sun which would soon be setting beyond the park in the distance. Seconds later, I was rushing back inside again. The dogs were parading anonymously at Monmore Green. No replay, no chance to confirm the worst, which was not that the horse had lost, or that it would have won had it got a run at that vital moment when switched to the rails - but that the dream had died, and that all those prospects of glory and freedom and vindication had gone in the wind. A ghostly voice whispered the result of the photograph. You could hear it in the background before it was properly transmitted. My horse had lost and I made for home.

Summary

We have resolved only to bet when in a positive frame of mind and have acknowledged that negative thoughts are inevitably punished in betting. Our aim is to develop a suitable betting style and a method of form study which will enable us quickly to identify the most promising betting opportunities on a day's cards. We realise there are no short-cuts in form analysis. At least an hour must be taken over each race and every runner studied in sequence. We must not be swayed by idle fancies. The horses we choose will have shown themselves to be capable of winning the race we are studying. They will quite probably be 'momentum' horses from stables in form. We will not be swayed by gossip masquerading as inside information, nor following the herd in backing obvious selections.

Now is the time to make our minds up which of these horses we will be taking with us to the next stage. The next stage, it should be noted, is not the visit to the betting shop, the racecourse or short walk across to the telephone. The next stage is not the striking of a bet. Incredibly, for many, it will be. They will have no concern for the next section of this book at all. They will give it not a moment's serious thought.

It never ceases to amaze me how many seemingly intelligent punters cannot, or will not, appreciate that there is another vital stage to the betting process, perhaps the most vital stage, still to be undergone after you have arrived at your fancies. Just as a batsman would not go out to the middle to face a fast bowler without the requisite pads, helmet and other gear, so should a punter not strike a bet without paying the closest attention to the facet of betting discussed in the next section, namely the assessment of value.

Odds As Percentages

Odds against	Price	Odds on
50.00	Evens	50.00
47.62	11-10	52.38
44.44	5-4	55.56
42.11	11-8	57.89
40.00	6-4	60.00
38.10	13-8	61.90
36.36	7-4	63.64
34.78	15-8	65.22
33.33	2-1	66.67
30.77	9-4	69.23
28.67	5-2	71.43
26.67	11-4	73.33
25.00	3-1	75.00
23.08	10-3	76.92
22.22	7-2	77.78
20.00	4-1	80.00
18.18	9-2	81.82
16.67	5-1	83.33
15.39	11-2	84.61
14.29	6-1	85.71
12.50	7-1	87.50
11.11	8-1	89.89
9.09	10-1	90.91
7.69	12-1	92.31
5.88	16-1	94.12
4.76	20-1	95.24
3.85	25-1	96.15
2.94	33-1	97.06
1.96	50-1	98.04
0.99	100-1	99.01

stage **three**

assessing value

Hint 31: Tell yourself: value is everything

It is the central premise of this book that we fail to win as much as we should at betting because of bad habits. But the bottom line, as the bookmakers might say, is we fail to win as much as we should because we do not obtain value for money on our selections. Value is all. The best habit any of us could acquire would be to ensure we obtain value for money on every selection we make. Unfortunately, of all the suggestions in this book, this one is far easier talked or written about than put into practice. Now is not the place to look in detail at the nuts and bolts of value betting. This I tried to do in the book of the same name.

What we must try to do here is to capitalise upon our insights into the subject. But a few basic reminders need not go amiss. Top sportsmen spend many more hours on the practice ground than they do in open competition and we backers could take the hint. Our problem is that we spend nearly all our time 'in the field' and far too little reflecting on our performance and refining our technique.

Hint 32: Think chances

Most punters spend the overwhelming majority of their betting time looking for the winner of a race and this is why they fail. They fail because this overly simplistic method of thinking contains its own booby trap which the majority proceed to detonate at their own expense. These backers usually end up backing what they consider is the most likely winner of a race. By definition, this is more often than not the favourite. If you back favourites on anything other than the most selective basis you are destined to lose, and lose horribly.

Most punters are not selective. QED - we must think chances and we must do so at a not inconsiderable level of subtlety and refinement. Every horse has a chance of winning any race for which it is entered, even a selling plater in the Derby. The horse's chance can be measured in terms of odds and percentages, listed in the following table. Every backer should familiarise themselves with these figures and understand their significance.

When we toss a coin we can say with something approaching certainty that the true chance of either heads or tails occurring on a single spin is even-money, or 50 per cent. I say 'something approaching certainty' because no doubt a scientist could undertake an analysis of the weight of the coin and note some infinitesimal imbalance which tilts matters fractionally in favour of heads or tails.

A nicety maybe, but it was precisely this type of thinking which enabled a group of professional gamblers to guarantee a profit on that most punter-unfriendly of games, roulette. With 36 numbers, plus the house zero, it would appear that the true chance of any one number resulting on a single spin is 36-1. With the house paying only 35-1 a nominated number, it would also seem clear that such a long-term roulette backer is effectively dead in the water.

However, I am told there used to be a brand of roulette wheel in circulation which was prone to inconsistencies in the make and shape of the 'diamonds' - the small metal shapes positioned above the numbers which alter the course of the ball as it circulates. Some of these diamonds were prone to become loose. If the ball made contact with one of those loose diamonds, it was likely to slow or stop more quickly than when knocking against the more secure ones, thus making it a good deal more likely to fall into one of the numbers beneath. The backers would support half a dozen strategically-positioned numbers 'against the field' in full expectation that the normally rock-solid house percentage was now in their favour!

Now, a horse race is clearly a different proposition to a toss of a coin or spin of a wheel because the true chance of each horse in each race cannot be verified. Perhaps there is a fiendish computer genius hoping to write a program to cover every conceivable eventuality, but the sheer weight of data is sure to defeat him. Value cannot be scientifically verified, it can only be intuited. And intuited only by the trained mind. It is interesting to draw an analogy with the philosophy of Plato and his 'theory of forms'. Information which is accessible to us in the everyday world, thought Plato, is but a pale imitation of its ultimate form, in the way that opinion is but a shadow of knowledge, and illusion inferior to belief. The philosopher was to occupy a privileged position in Plato's society because, through the proper application of the disciplines of his craft, notably the application of reason, he could rise above illusion and belief and, quite literally, gaze upon the truth.

The vision of the ultimate truth which disciplined backers are seeking is the true price of each horse. (The undisciplined backer, meanwhile, remains firmly rooted in the world of illusion and opinion.) Maybe there is no prospect of being able to gaze directly upon these prices in the Platonic Value Heaven (cynics no doubt suggesting they are zealously guarded by some supra-sensible Tom Kelly figure, clad in white), but surely we can intuit them. Think of those times when you struck a bet convinced you were taking a value price. In essence, you were believing - indeed you knew - that the true price of your horse was less than the actual price you had obtained.

The Macs Maharanee bet I referred to earlier would be one such example from my recent betting experience. Based on the evidence gathered, I was convinced the horse was no bigger than a 4-1 chance. Convinced to a point of certainty. When 7-1 was available in the morning lists, I needed no persuading to step in for as much as would be accepted. As revealed earlier, sadly, and unluckily, Macs Maharanee lost, being caught on the line by Blue Topaze, who had finished with such a wet sail she should have been entered for the next race at Cowes. But I left the betting shop that evening knowing, with utter certainty, that if every bet I struck was of the quality of Macs Maharanee I could not fail to win in the future.

Of course it was impossible to verify my intuition about the true chance of Macs Maharanee, just as it will be impossible for you to do so when you are next in a similar, happy position - but the strength of feeling was sufficient to suggest I was at least close to a vision of the truth.

Hint 33: Ask yourself: what price am I prepared to take for my fancy?

A backer who thinks in terms of chance has to think in terms of price because the two are interlinked. After we have assessed the form credentials of each horse in the race, it is time to ask yourself what price you are prepared to take for you fancy? Or, expressed more fully, what is the minimum value price you are prepared to accept for this selection? In my book *Value Betting*, I included a method for translating form credentials into prices which has often helped me pin-point winners. I believe this method holds good, but a number of readers have expressed difficulty in understanding the system. I have since decided that there is an easier, if equally time-consuming way to undertake the vital matter of price assessment, and it involves reference to the starting-price (SP) of each horse.

Now the problem with the SP, of course, is that it is not revealed until a race is off; until after the reporters have gone into their huddle and agreed on the state of the market at the off. Many backers complain the system is intrinsically unfair and that there is sometimes a kind of conspiracy to shorten the SP of certain horses, especially those who are strongly fancied. I have no sympathy with backers holding these views.

Although it may look suspicious when a well-backed winner's SP is lower than the final show, the figures suggest this happens only in a minority of cases and that almost as many winners are returned at a longer price than their final show. And in the hurly-burly of the ring, when the representatives of the big bookmakers are often scuttling around shortening horses as the stalls are filling, there is often insufficient time for prices to be relayed to the shops via SIS. The system is certainly not perfect, but backers have one simple and direct response. It is worth a hint in its own right.

Hint 34: Never back at starting-price

We don't take goods off the shelf unless we know the price, so why should we do so with our bets? Backers who moan about a lower than expected SP are directing their venom at the wrong target. They should be asking themselves why they did not take a price when they had the chance. It may be a disgrace that the big bookmakers are able to manipulate the on-course market as they do, free from any procedures to ensure accountability, but this is an unpalatable fact of life, not an excuse for whingeing when we end up with the thin end of the wedge on our SP bet.

Those in doubt about the wisdom of taking SP should consider the following imaginary four-runner race in which each horse has an equal chance. The true price for each horse will be 3-1, taking 25 per cent out of the book, with a total take-out of 100 per cent. The problem is no self-respecting bookmaker is going to post these prices, for he has no edge. (This can be verified by noting that an equal stake on each runner would return the backer's money, whoever the winner.)

Bookmakers, being the creatures they are, must have their profit margin, or over-round.

Imaginary race: true prices

HORSE A:	3-1	25.00	
HORSE B:	3-1	25.00	
HORSE C:	3-1	25.00	
HORSE D:	3-1	25.00	100.00

Let us assume that, on this occasion, they have been made aware that the true price for each horse is 3-1. (Even Ladbrokes' information network hasn't reached this level of efficiency but no doubt they are working on it.) When it comes to pricing up the race, they will open up something like this:

Imaginary race: opening show

HORSE A:	5-2	28.67	
HORSE B:	5-2	28.67	
HORSE C:	5-2	28.67	
HORSE D:	5-2	28.67	114.68

Assuming a tenner is staked on each horse at these prices, and nothing more, then the bookmaker is in the happy position of being unable to lose. He will take £40 and return £35, giving him a profit margin of 12.5 per cent. Now it is a truth not widely acknowledged that the bookmakers nearly always give themselves a greater profit margin on the opening show than will prevail at the end of the betting on a race. (They like to test the water at the outset and there are always a few mugs on hand who must, simply must, take the opening show.)

If in doubt, tot up the over-round on the next first show you see in your betting shop, then check with the figure given in the *Racing Post* returns the following day.

The chances are the SP percentage will be more favourable to the punter, if only marginally. (If still in doubt, note how many horses drift from the first show compared with those who shorten.) If nothing else, therefore, the blind backer is better off taking SP than plunging in for the first show. But we are not in the business of betting blind, nor of settling for SP. At the end of the betting on our imaginary four-runner race, the starting-prices returned might look something like this:

Imaginary race: starting-prices

HORSE A:	5-2	28.67	
HORSE B:	11-4	26.67	
HORSE C:	11-4	26.67	
HORSE D:	11-4	26.67	108.68

The prices will have been shortened or lengthened according to weight of money. Clearly, SP backers will not have obtained value for money on any selection in this race. In fact, we may assume few punters did obtain any value - though some were successful, as can be seen by noting the best price available for any of the horses during the course of betting on the race.

Imaginary race: best prices available

HORSE A:	11-4	26.67	
HORSE B:	11-4	26.67	
HORSE C:	3-1	25.00	
HORSE D:	100-30	23.08	101.42

Those shrewd and quick enough to have taken some of the 100-30 offered for Horse D, will have obtained value for money on their selection. This we can verify by noting that the true price is shorter, at 3-1. Again, if one were to tot up the percentages on the best prices available at any time for each horse in a race, the sum will always be shorter than that recorded by the SPs, sometimes considerably so. (On rare occasions the total over-round will come to less than 100 per cent, putting the margin in the punters' favour.)

On this occasion, let us assume Horse A wins and Horse D finishes a poor last of the four runners. SP backers of A, blissfully unaware of their folly, pat themselves on the back and prepare another selection. They enjoy a joke at the expense of the punter who took the 100-30 about Horse D, who is doing his best to persuade them that he had the value. "A 5-2 winner beats a 100-30 loser any day in our book," laugh the Horse A backers. Of course, anybody can be proved right in the short-term. It is only in the long-term that they tend to be exposed for the fools they are.

Let us assume that the above race is run 100 times. It is reasonable to expect that each horse will win 25 of the races. (Statistics seldom pan out this perfectly, but we can assume so for our purposes.) Let us see how SP backers fare on each of the four horses, assuming they have a level £10 stake on each of the 100 races.

	Total staked	SP	Total return
HORSE A:	£1,000	5-2	£875.00
HORSE B:	£1,000	11-4	£937.50
HORSE C:	£1,000	11-4	£937.50
HORSE D:	£1,000	11-4	£937.50

Twenty-five of the 100 £10 bets struck win, so the total return is the equivalent of a £250 bet at the relevant SP. An unhappy scenario for backers of any of the four horses. But unrealistic perhaps? Manufactured for the sake of argument? Hardly, I'm afraid. Reality for SP backers is considerably more gloomy. The total SP percentage in our example (108.68) is perfectly realistic for a four-runner race. (A decent rule of thumb is to assume two points over-round for every runner in a race up to 12 runners, then one point thereafter. Thus, the figure for a 10-runner race will be 120, for a 18-runner race 130, and so on.)

As can be deduced from the above, the bigger the field the worse the SP backer is likely to fare. Even in our race, backers of any of the four runners will have needed to have been extremely lucky to have broken even. Nearly all SP betting is done off-course.

Assuming tax is paid on, backers will therefore have had to return £1,100 in order to break even. We have agreed that 25 is the average number of wins for each horse in our 100-race example. This is the number of wins SP backers needed in order to break even.

HORSE A:	32
HORSE B:	30
HORSE C:	30
HORSE D:	30

Backers of Horses B-D will have needed to buck the average by 20 per cent in order to break even; backers of Horse A required a 28 per cent swing in their favour. By contrast, anybody backing the even chances at roulette needs to buck the average by around 1.4 per cent in order to break even. Few, if any, long-term roulette punters have ever managed to come out in front. So what chance SP backers? You have been warned.

For the purposes of the example, let us return to consider the fate of the backer who took the 100-30. In the first example, he lost. But assume he managed to obtain 100-30 Horse D in each of the 100 races.

	Total staked	Price obtained	Total return
HORSE D:	£1,000	100-30	£1,083.33

A healthy profit, although it is worth noting how the imposition of betting tax would wipe it out altogether. But who said the game was easy?

Hint 35: Always aim to beat starting-price, plus 20 per cent

If we are not going to take SP, you might be asking, why worry about it? I think we should worry about it because it is one of the best guides we have to the true chance of a horse in a race. Of course, the SP will nearly always be shorter than the true price, given the over-round. A useful test in all but the biggest fields is to try to ensure that you secure better than SP, plus 20 per cent. Thus, if SP is to be 4-1, you should aim to secure at least 4.8-1 to your money. If SP is to be 6-1, you should aim for at least 7.2-1. If SP is to be 10-1, you should aim for at least 12-1. And so on. If you manage to succeed in passing this test on a regular basis, you will not be going too far wrong, I can assure you.

Hint 36: Learn how to compile a betting forecast

In order to take advantage of Hint 34, it is essential to be able to form an accurate assessment of the likely SP. Assessing SPs is a skill few punters can boast, but one which it is one well worth acquiring. I have always believed the ability of a tipster is best gleaned not from his or her ability to pick winners, but from the accuracy of their betting or SP forecast.

You may not have been aware that it is the job of the Spotlight and Man On The Spot writer in the two racing dailies not only to discuss the races at his or her meeting - but also to compile the betting forecast. In my experience, this is most definitely the most difficult part of the job, and perhaps one which is not given enough emphasis. The glory, after all, is in tipping or (better still) napping a winner.

When writing the Pricewise column, I always tried to predict the likely SP of the horse I was recommending in order that backers could form an idea of the level of value they were obtaining at the morning price, and I took as much personal satisfaction in making an accurate price assessment as in tipping a big winner. I believe all backers should make the attempt to compile a betting forecast, for it can often highlight the accuracy, or otherwise, of one's opinions.

So how to begin the task? Much, it has to be said, depends upon a combination of experience and following one's intuition. But here's a rough guide:

1) Aim for the prices of the first six in your betting show to tot up to 100 per cent. (Many bookmakers use this rule of thumb, so why shouldn't we?)

2) Try to identify the likely favourite in the race. (This will not always be as easy as it seems.)

3) Ask yourself at which price you would become interested in backing the horse.

4) Deduct 20 per cent from this price.

5) Ask yourself whether there are any reasons why the horse might be even more heavily backed (e.g. is it a popular horse with the betting public, or ridden by a top jockey?). If so, shorten the price again, perhaps by as much as 10 per cent.

6) You now have a favourite, and a price for the favourite. (Both, of course, might be hideously wrong, but only experience will help here).

7) Compare the chance of your second-favourite with the favourite. Try to make a transfer into prices. (If, for instance, you reckon your favourite has double the chance of your second-favourite and the former is assessed at 2-1 (take out 33.33), your second-favourite should be put in at 5-1 (take-out 16.67).

8) Try to quote the first six in the betting, if not all horses - and, of course, the price for any horse you may be interested in backing.

9) Tot up your over-round.

10) Make any adjustments, up or down, to aim to fulfil step 1 above.

11) Scan your list. Does it have an authentic ring to it?

12) Be prepared, in theory, to be willing to lay any of your horses at the price quoted. In other words, play bookmaker.

13) Compare your effort with the betting forecast in the *Racing Post* or *Sporting Life*. Perhaps also your evening or daily paper, though their forecasts will be considerably less reliable.

14) Are there any glaring differences?

15) Who do you trust, yourself or the writer?

16) Make any necessary adjustments.

17) Have a look at the selection box in both daily papers. This will often give invaluable help (a pity it is generally not available to Spotlight writers because of tight deadlines; howlers could sometimes be avoided.)

18) Taking the *Racing Post* box for the example, it is a fair rule of thumb that if a horse is the unanimous selection of each tipster it is almost certain to start odds-on. Also a horse with at least two more selections than its nearest rival will probably start favourite. A horse with five or more selections is most unlikely to start above the 6-1 mark. A horse with two selections is most unlikely to start above 14-1.

The above guide is intended as a starter's guide for compiling betting forecasts. Do have a try. With time, you will begin to get a feel for the business and no doubt be able to put my tips aside in favour of your own methods!

Hint 37: Betting forecasts: a danger point

Before you compile a betting forecast, you will almost certainly have an idea in your head of the price you are hoping to be able to snap up for your fancy in a race. More often than not, as you are in the process of compiling the forecast, you will become aware that you are most unlikely to be able to obtain the price you have earmarked for your selection. This is a danger point. Just as nobody likes to spend an hour working on a race only to find that no selection stands out as betting material, so nobody likes to become excited at the prospect of backing a horse, only to find that the hoped-for price will be unavailable.

Now, the discipline involved in compiling the forecast will nearly always help you to refine your early assessment. In order to reach an accurate forecast, you will no doubt have quickly reviewed each horse's form. Perhaps you will spot a couple of points which eluded you in earlier analysis. In such circumstances, you may decide that you were too conservative in your earlier estimate. Perhaps you had earmarked 5-1 as the price at which you would become interested in backing a horse.

But, on further analysis, the level of opposition seems to be weaker than you had considered. In such circumstances, you might judge it appropriate to reduce the minimum value price to 4-1. Equally, you might judge the opposition to be stronger and extend the first assessment to 6-1 or even longer.

Perhaps, however, your initial assessment of the minimum value price holds (as one would often expect it to do), and your betting forecast suggests it will not be available. You are now disappointed and faced with a temptation. The temptation to cheat. To cheat yourself. To think, perhaps I was being too cautious in my initial assessment. I thought 4-1 was the minimum value price, but it is really more like 3-1. Or thoughts to this effect. No doubt there will be the prospect of taking an interest at the 3-1, thus rewarding your labours. Censor these thoughts. Dismiss them from your mind. These days, more than ever, the backer needs to cultivate one quality more than most - DETACHMENT. This is the first of my three D's for successful betting. The others are DISCIPLINE and DEDICATION. A hint on this matter, just to drive it home.

Hint 38: Beware of 'the pull of the action'

At the heart of the appeal of gambling lies 'the action'. The word itself acts as a spur to the gambler, speaking of movement, excitement, adrenalin and involvement. It is hard to resist the lure of the action. This explains why we often take the 3-1 about the horse we know in our heart to be no better than a 4-1 chance. We simply cannot bear not to be involved. In no other place in the world are so many people hell-bent on leaving the real world behind and getting in on the action than in Las Vegas. Here is Anthony Holden's experience, described in *Big Deal: One Year As A Professional Poker Player*.

"From the air ... there's an hour or so of infinite desert to savour from a safe seat above, with the misty imaginings of the wagon trains of the old frontiersmen, and of certain death facing anyone wandering down there right now, before you catch your first extraordinary, breathtaking glimpse of this clutch of fantastical towers and glass palaces slapped down at random in the middle of this moonscape, this vast and utter nowhere ... Touchdown and disembarkation are your last, brief contacts with reality before entering a world like no other on earth, where all normal values swiftly evaporate, all lifelong interests and enthusiasms erode, and all curiosity about the outside world is absently abandoned - overmastered by the Siren Song of life in the fast lane."

Professionals as well as occasional gamblers find the action hard to resist. In the words of former world poker champion 'Amarillo Slim' Preston: "I go anywhere for a big game because I thrive on action. Don't get me wrong - I like the money, too - but it's the challenge and thrill of matching wits with and beating the best poker players in the world that turns me on."

Poker players have a word for those who cannot cope with the action, who become disorientated and throw all judgment to the wind. They are said to be 'on tilt'. Most of us, most of the time, gamble on tilt. We're not quite in control. We might think we are, but we're not. Until my summer of betting in 1993, I used to think I had the game under control. After 15 years of serious betting, I thought I could make it pay, that I could find a good winner when I needed one. Now I know that my betting, although relatively successful, has been spoiled by bad habits, carelessness and laziness. Hence this book and an attempt to drive those habits from the system. Not that it will be easy. Most punters are like Pavlov's dog - we're conditioned.

Consider the British betting shop. These places are open six days a week, 52 weeks a year, barring the odd bank holiday. Inside, customers are barraged with a ceaseless flow of information: prices, results, news, views, tips and special offers. The schedules have been fine-tuned to ensure a race is run every five or so minutes, horses or dogs. You can bet on everything from Epsom to Elvis returning. You can bet singles or doubles, starting-price or board price, win or each-way, Tote or SP. Multi-coloured, fast-changing screens convey the action. Talk is constant. It is all planned, every last detail, even down to the employment of Derek Thompson. The aim is to relieve the current captive audience of as much of their money as possible in the shortest available time.

The accountants who run the big firms want us dashing around like headless chickens, unsure whether to peck at Salisbury, Hackney or Monmore Green - or maybe at a combination of all three. ("Why not try an across-the-card double here at Ladbrokes. We'll offer you a 10 per cent bonus!") Whilst it is certainly easy to shun these special offers - if a bookmaker is conceding 10 per cent, you can rest assured he has another 50 safely secured under his sleeve - it is far more difficult to stand aloof from the action. The bookmakers call the recent changes to the betting environment 'progress', allowing them to 'enhance customer service' - and to an extent they have a point. Betting shops, on the whole, are more agreeable places to spend an afternoon than in the days when spit and sawdust ruled.

Believe it not, when satellite television was first introduced into the betting shops in 1987, the bookmakers were worried men. They feared the actual sight of their money going down might entice customers to become more discriminating with their wagers. Perhaps also they might choose to sit back in their seats and watch the racing without having a bet. Damn it, the bookmakers were even providing the seats.

So together with their Satellite Information Services (SIS), in whom they had invested heavily, and with the full co-operation of the Levy Board and the Jockey Club's race planning department (it is they who schedule the impossible-to-fathom handicap at the end of every card), the big bookmakers set out to create the hectic, all-action, bingo-style atmosphere you now find in your local betting shop, all the way down to employing their own, in-house flunky to jolly everybody along in the manner of a Butlin's redcoat.

The bookmakers wanted to ensure it would be all but impossible to get your bearings in a betting shop. They wanted to disorientate those customers who planned to come in for one bet and then leave the shop. They wanted to entice them to remain, to stick around, just like the regulars. We punters, being adaptable beings, have on the whole fallen for the strategy. We have been conditioned. I, for one, miss the atmosphere of an old-style betting shop, even the infamous Extel commentaries.

Nowadays we worry about the influence the big bookmakers have on SIS, but we should not forget how the Extel men were briefed to give the favourite a favourable mention, however badly it was faring; and how the final furlong of a race would often take up to a minute and a half in order that almost every horse in the field could be heard with a chance.

We lived in hope in those days, ear cocked to the crackly tannoy in the corner, awaiting a mention for our fancy. When it came, when we were noted making progress on the leaders, there was a surge, a fix of adrenalin, which is somehow missing now. You could let your imagination do the work, for nobody knew what was happening in those days, only Extel themselves. Who can forget waiting, after they had "gone past together" for the numbers to be announced in the photo-finish. Who can forget the enticing delays before the delivery. "A photograph... photograph... between number nine Secreto and number four El Gran Senor."

When your number was called first you relaxed, for they did not often get the order wrong. The first called usually won. I guess that on the odd occasion the delay was so great the result had already been announced on the course.

During the wait for the result of one photo-finish, a middle-aged man once turned to me and pronounced, with statesmanlike assurance, that the horse called first in a photograph always won. I begged to correct him, pointing out that the order only represented the opinion of the Extel man on the course. "Doesn't matter," he confided. "In all the years I've been betting I've never known a horse called second be named the winner."

Moments later, of course, the second horse got it, and the man turned to me with a bewildered look in his eyes and I was sorry I had argued with him, as if I had somehow helped to hasten the demise of the only certainty he had ever known. What do such men believe in now, when you can see at a glance that your horse is palpably outpaced, outclassed or, worse, out the back, taking it easy? Even the winners can have a sting in the tail, as you watch them cruise to the line, knowing you should have had another fifty on at least. In the Extel days, when everything was heard but nothing was seen, you were free to dream. Anything might happen and probably did.

Nostalgia perhaps, but there must be something in it. I am willing to wager I am not the only punter who, faced with the choice of a telephone commentary or a short walk to the betting shop, will pick up the phone and listen, knuckles white. These days we get Graham, Aussie Jim, Simon or even Derek, instead of the regional crooners Extel would employ, in order that their accent fitted the locale - in the Midlands, a Brummie; in the North-East, a Geordie. You remember, they were almost friends.

But the thrill is still there, the hope, burning freshly, that your horse, who is yet to be mentioned, is at this very moment preparing to unleash a spectacular challenge. Extel provided action. Maybe the game was just as organised in those days, maybe we were as manipulated, as conditioned, by the pauses in the Extel commentaries, those terrifying little delays on which fortunes turned. Maybe. But I sometimes wonder if the big bookmakers, in their ceaseless quest for profits, are not squeezing all the fun out of the game.

Gambling depends upon anticipation, upon the prospect of striking it big. If this is lost, what remains? The action, of course. Most people must know they will never make a profit from their betting, but they keep coming back. They'd like to win, but they don't have the time. Anyway, who says the appeal of gambling lies only in the money we might win?

The famous poker player Nick 'The Greek' Dandalos ("The next best thing to gambling and winning is gambling and losing...") used to play for tens of thousands a time, but ended broke, hustling the tourists at the two-bit tables. "It's action, isn't it?" was his ready justification.

Summary:

We first compiled a list of horses whose chance caught our eye. Then we proceeded to assess whether any of those horses were likely to represent value for money. We started to think in terms of prices and chances, reaching an idea of the minimum value price we will be prepared to take about a selection.

Some will have followed the 'Form and Value System' listed in *Value Betting*. Others will have chosen to compile a betting forecast. This will have given them a hopefully accurate guide to the likely starting-price of each runner in a race, certainly of the first six in the betting. Those compiling such forecasts will have been in a position to take advantage of the hint to "beat starting-price plus 20 per cent". We will not have weakened our resolve when it becomes clear we will not be able to obtain the price we require for our selection. We will not have been lured into the action. We shall only have been prepared to play when all the factors are in our favour, as far as we can judge.

stage **four**

preparing to bet

Hint 39: Find the appropriate type of bet for your selection(s)

There are almost as many types of bet available to the British punter as there are horses in training. This is the fabled 'choice' which apologists for our flawed betting system tend to cite to justify its (and their) existence. I am of the view that nobody would miss the Union Jack or the Heinz or the Goliath if they were scrapped. No doubt plenty would rue the departure of the Yankee, Lucky 15 or Tricast, but only in the manner in which an ex-smoker craves for a cigarette. These bets are a habit best kicked. Hence...

Hint 40: Avoid extravagant multiple bets

It's an old chestnut this one, but it clearly bears repeating, for the special slip dispensers for these bets are nearly always halfway empty whenever I visit a betting shop. I use the word 'extravagant' because there are times when a cleverly-planned multiple bet, or series of multiple bets, can be potentially rewarding. I list three such examples below:

1) Each-way doubles: A real 'thieving' bet, which the bookmakers hate and often refuse to accept. Never strike this bet unless you are convinced you are getting value for money on the place element of the bet. Treat the win part as a bonus.

2) Tricasts: A hopeless bet for the everyday punter but occasionally worth

considering when you have picked out three or four against the field in a big handicap with at least 12 runners. If you feel these rivals are clearly superior but you cannot separate them for the purpose of win singles, it can be worth trying a small-stake combination Tricast. The Tricast can also appeal when the draw is conveying a large advantage in big fields. Keep an eye on results to discover trends.

3)   Forecasts: In the case of the three or four against the field, it will be safer - and probably wiser - to combine the selections in forecasts. More dramatically, if you believe you have identified two horses as clearly superior against the field, the forecast can be dynamite. The choice will be between the bookmaker's computer straight-forecast (reversed if necessary) and the Tote's dual-forecast. The latter tends to offer much the better value for bigger-priced selections, although the pools are often so small a decent-sized bet will spoil the dividend. Some off-course bookmakers accept Tote dual-forecasts, but watch their limits and exclusion clauses.

I know of one exceptionally good judge who is fond of mixed trebles (i.e. he has two selections in each of three races chosen and combines them in eight trebles) but you need to have a rare confidence in your own ability to follow this kind of strategy. In theory, if you have value on a number of selections, then the value will be enhanced if you combine them in multiple bets. But you will often have to wait a long time for your pay-off and will need to ensure consistency in staking in order not to miss the big pay-day. (For more on this vital point see Stage Five.) There are two multiple bets which can offer such remarkable value on occasions that I wish to recommend them in separate hints.

Hint 41: Study the Tote Jackpot meeting when there is a carry over of more than £50,000

Normally, it is difficult for most of us to find one winner, let alone six in sequence, but when there is enough of a carrot in terms of money carried over, then it is worth taking a pot-shot at the Jackpot. Due to inadequate marketing by the Tote, who have been entertaining this angel unawares for decades, the size of the Jackpot pool does not reach the above heights as often as it could. But when it does, it offers a chance for a spectacular pay-day. And, it should be said, for spectacular disappointments. I have won the Jackpot to relatively small money, but have missed out on the big win on at least four agonising occasions. The worst would have been at Goodwood in May 1983, when I had five winners and an unlucky second. The dividend came to over £15,000.

My tips are not to dilute your bet by having too many combinations - and to stay out if you find yourself unable to split five or six horses in one or more races. If all are included, no doubt you will find yourself having to pay for too many combinations (unless you have bankers elsewhere, when it might be worth chancing the six selections) and if you choose to leave out one, sod's law will come into operation and it will win - and quite probably go down in your own personal betting history as the last-second compromise which cost you a fortune.

Hint 42: Consider the Tote Placepot

This is one of my favourite bets, and I recommend it strongly. The key point is the amount of 'mug money' in the pool, staked by occasional racegoers who (understandably) find the bet a cheap and appealing one, and by suicide merchants who cannot stop themselves from combining 'favourites through the card', and who should know better. Apparently around 10 per cent of all Placepots are favourites through the card, which proves there is more than one born every minute. The dividend will almost always disappoint if all the favourites are placed.

Again, each backer will have his own favourite strategy for this bet - and it is sufficiently flexible not to accommodate many different approaches. (Most of the Placepot strategies I have read about seem unduly conservative for my taste, for instance by combining first and second favourites in combinations, but their exponents swear by them.) Nevertheless here are a few suggestions.

1) Treat the bet as a serious entity, not as a casual sideline. (I will admit I have been rewarded for last-minute Placepots in the past, and have often taken a 'just for fun' combination when I did not fancy a more serious effort. But this sort of betting remains in the realm of the unprofessional and I intend to eliminate it after an extremely poor 1993 season with the casual Placepot. This sort of lazy betting inevitably catches up with you and is bad for the soul.

2) As with the Jackpot, don't water down your bet with too many combinations. I would have thought 64 combinations (representing two selections in each race) was an absolute maximum - and I like to chisel the

bet down to no more than 32, and hopefully fewer.

3) It helps to have at least one, if not more bankers on which you are prepared to rely.

4) Beware of six- and seven-runner races. These are often the trickiest in which to find a placed horse.

5) Don't feel you have to stick to a maximum of £1 per line.

6) In order to protect your dividend it is best to spread your Placepots around off-course, although be prepared for your bookmaker to be profoundly suspicious and watch his limits.

7) That noted, always ensure your combinations are represented in the Tote pool in order to avoid the nightmare of holding winning tickets when no dividend is declared.

8) As above again, be prepared for shattering disappointment. Last spring, I had prepared what I considered to be a rock-solid Placepot for the first day of the Goodwood May Meeting. Four combinations at £20 a line. When I was writing out one of the slips in a Chichester betting shop, I spotted there was a non-runner in the first race. This reduced the field to seven, meaning my banker in this race, which was Jaazim, now needed to finish in the first two and not the first three, a considerable extra burden. I considered adding a second choice in Simply Finesse, but decided against it. It would have meant diluting my bet to £10 a line - and I had faith in Jaazim, who was trained by my old ally Dick Hern.

The decision not to include Simply Finesse in my combinations was to cost me over £18,000. He beat a 66-1 shot in the first race, with Jaazim running a tired fourth. As soon as the runners passed the line I knew the gambling gods were in a particularly spiteful mood. Was it not 10 years to the day when I had nearly won over £8,000 with a 50p Jackpot combination? Of course I did not know after that first race that history was going to repeat itself in such a diabolical manner.

But I suspected it strongly, indeed I predicted as much to myself, as I walked to view the runners in the paddock for the next race. All my enthusiasm for the day's racing had evaporated. I decided to expend all my energy on getting the Placepot I could (should?) have placed beaten, on restoring equilibrium by grimly willing my selections out of the frame.

You will not believe this, but there are witnesses to confirm that I had also picked out four horses as possible value propositions that afternoon. They were Pistol River (won 7-1), Geisway (won 9-2), Red Bishop (won 5-1) and Reflecting (won 10-1). The last three were trained by John Gosden, whose stable I had resolved to follow that season. I backed none of those horses. To be honest, I don't think I ever recovered from this day last season, which is not to make an excuse, but merely to show that strange and powerful forces can sometimes surround our betting and we had better be aware of their existence.

Jung had a term for amazing coincidences, which he liked to study. He called it synchronicity. Such coincidences, he thought, communicated meaning in ways not open to our regular thought processes. It was at the time of this Placepot that I was just becoming aware things were not going to work out on my summer of betting. At that point, I had not logged into the reasons why I was destined to fail, which I now realise were linked to bad habits developed over the years.

Perhaps this coincidence, or merely the loss itself, was a way of allowing me to get on top of this point. A meaningful coincidence in the Jungian mould? Or just one of those things? Who knows. But one thing is certain. The Placepot remains a superb bet and don't let my experience put you off getting involved in it on a regular basis.

Hint 43: Consider ante-post betting

Although there remains a suspicion that a good deal of the value has been squeezed from the ante-post market, this is a form of betting which every punter should consider including in his or her portfolio. Many of my most memorable winning bets were struck ante-post, notably Nashwan at 33-1 for both the 2,000 Guineas and Derby, but also Don't Forget Me (33-1 for the 1987 2,000 Guineas), Hallo Dandy (33-1 for the 1984 Grand National) and Sun Princess (33-1 for the 1983 Oaks). Some notable near-misses as well, of course, notably Alnasr Alwasheek (33-1 for the 1992 2,000 Guineas), Belmez (40-1 for the 1990 Derby) and Unfuwain (40-1 for the 1988 Derby), who were all favourites for the race at some stage, but missed out. Ante-post betting can be divided into three areas:

1) Long-term bets. These will be struck at least a month and conceivably years in advance on the Championship events - the Flat classics and the Gold Cup and Champion Hurdle over jumps. They require an act of faith in the selection getting to post and of course the backer can have no idea of the strength of the field at the time of staking. Nashwan for the Derby was one such bet. I first backed him in August 1988, nearly 10 months before the race.

2)   Medium-term bets. With these bets it will be possible to make a reasoned calculation of the chance of a selection making it to post, and there will be some idea of the likely make-up of the race. For instance, backing a horse for a classic after it has run well in a trial. Or backing a horse for a big handicap on publication of the weights.

3)   Short-term bets. These will be struck up to five days in advance, when the five-day declarations have been made known. Of particular interest are the big Saturday jumps handicaps in the first half of the season, such as the Mackeson and Hennessy Gold Cups. I enjoyed a number of memorable coups on these races in my Pricewise days, notably with Beau Ranger (1987 Mackeson) and Ghofar (1989 Hennessy).

These can all be classed as ante-post bets, because you lose your money if they fail to get to post. This is the downside. The upside to ante-post betting is the chance to obtain a significantly larger price about your selection than will be available to those backing nearer the off. Let this point be stressed. To my mind there is little point in backing ante-post at the sort of price which is available for a solid favourite running in half an hour. I am thinking here of a number of the recent ante-post classic favourites such as Zafonic and Sayyedati. Yes, I know these two were victorious, but this does not exonerate those backers who stepped in for the extremely short prices which were available over the winter.

I don't think it is simply nostalgia for the good old days which leads to the conclusion that much of the value has gone in the ante-post market, particularly on the classics. The problem is publicity. The media take a much more active role in reporting ante-post betting than they did, say, 10 years ago, with the result that many more punters are getting involved. This, in turn, means that the big firms have to be more wary of their liabilities than in the old days, when they used the ante-post book to 'mark their card' about the likely outcome of a big race.

Ante-post betting also gives the big firms a chance to see their name up in lights - and they do not waste any time, tending to quote 20-1 for the Guineas or Derby about almost every maiden winner from one of the big stables. This is not to say it is no longer possible to get 33-1 about a horse with sound claims who has the potential to start a rock-solid favourite on the day. You simply have to look a good deal harder - and be patient, discerning and shrewd.

As ever, try not to run with the pack. If there are reports in your paper of a horse being heavily backed after working well at home, nod sagely to yourself and turn the page. If nothing else, the top price will have gone and you will be left to pick up the pieces. And home work is a notoriously bad guide to racecourse performance, although it does give a chance for pundits like Derek Thompson to indicate how much they are in the know. Equally, don't be bounced into a bet after reading some excitable newspaper copy about a horse being well-handicapped for a forthcoming race. Form your own opinion before moving in.

Some other tips for ante-post betting:

1) Play bookmaker. Ask yourself what price you would be quoting after a horse has run in a trial. If your price is notably shorter than that reported, there may be a bet on.

2) Be sharp - the top prices seldom last long.

3) If you have missed the price you wanted, don't chase imaginary winnings by taking a shorter one. (For more advice on this vital point see Hint 54.)

4) Follow Hint 16 in this book. Ask yourself, is this the type of horse needed to win the race in question? Pay particular attention to the trainer's past performance in the race and the record of the trial as a future guide.

5) Stick with the top yards for the classics. It is impossible to imagine the equivalent of the 1990 Gold Cup hero Norton's Coin winning a 2,000 Guineas or Derby.

6) Pay particular attention to Flat trainers aiming at one of the top jumping prizes.

7) Seldom, if ever, bet ante-post if there is any doubt about your horse taking part even if it is in peak form. For example, have connections another race in mind? Does it require soft ground, or act only on a sound surface? Also does the owner have other options for the race? The Arabs have been a boon to British racing, but they have done nothing for the ante-post market. I still remember Khalid Abdulla pulling Rainbow Quest out of the 1984 Derby in order to run a one-paced plodder named Alphabatim. I'm still convinced the former would have won. Of course I'm speaking through my pocket, having taken 33-1 Rainbow Quest some months earlier, but who remembers the moderate winner Secreto - or, worse, the close third, Mighty Flutter? I am afraid I was guilty of falling into the same trap with Armiger in 1993. Even if the horse did not quite train on as expected, he had won the Chester Vase, only to be talked down in favour of the wretched Tenby. And what happened? The owner won with his third string, a horse unraced as a two-year-old. Let us hope Commander In Chief's success does not encourage a further trend away from racing horses

in a serious manner at two. After all, a hard season did not stop Dr Devious or Generous from claiming Derby glory on the first Wednesday in June.

8) Pay close attention to Michael Kinane's ride. This is not exactly an ante-post recommendation, for he is often only put up at the last moment, but his big-race record speaks for itself.

9) Be sure your horse will get the trip. This is of particular relevance to the Derby and Oaks but is sensible advice for any race.

10) Trust your intuition. Some horses ooze class and seem to advertise themselves as future champions. Anybody who saw Nashwan canter to post on his debut would have had an inkling that this was no ordinary racehorse. Sometimes, it seems, a performance makes a deep impression on you and you simply have to get involved. Think of Shergar's trials and the Channel 4 team after Zafonic in the Prix de la Salamandre. My they were boring about him, but any punter with an ante-post voucher burning a hole in his pocket is likely to be tedious company. I can still put people to sleep about Nashwan now, nearly five years after his great win. Ante-post betting is great fun. Unlike most bets, which are here today and gone tomorrow, ante-post selections are like friends. You become attached to them and care about their welfare. I am not one to join the sentimental school of racing journalism, but we all have our favourites. And if there is a better feeling in racing than watching your horse strike the front a furlong out, knowing you are full up to your maximum at 33-1 and prices downwards, then I am yet to hear about it.

Hint 44: Beware each-way betting

It is one of the most common mistakes in betting to compromise with an each-way bet. "I don't fancy it too strongly, so I'll back it each-way," would be the reasoning. We punters have our own peculiar way with logic, but this really does take the biscuit. Because we don't fancy a horse, we tell ourselves we plan to strike two bets instead of one or none; a bet for the win and a bet for the place. Do not think the likelihood of a horse being placed can compensate for any lack of value on the win element. If a horse is not value for the win, you should not be backing it and that is the end of the matter. To fiddle around with an each-way bet is to compound the felony.

You should only back each-way if you believe you are getting value for the win and value for the place. To take the point a stage further, I believe you should only back each-way if you cannot see the horse in question finishing out of the frame. In other words, if the race has the right 'shape' for each-way betting. I discuss this concept in greater detail in *Value Betting*, but an example might be if three horses are clearly superior to the rivals in an eight-runner race. If one of those horses is showing at 5-1 or better, it will probably be worth investigating an each-way bet, providing the horse represents value to win the race.

I am firmly of the view that almost every punter who resolved to stop backing each-way, and have the full stake on for the win instead, would find themselves better off in the long run. My results bear this out, and so do those of a number of respected judges whom I have consulted on the matter. It is a different matter to take a covering interest on the place if you are backing at long prices, say £200 over £50 on a 16-1 shot in a 12-runner race. But, once again, you should only take the place interest if you believe the odds (in this case 4-1) represent value and if you believe the £50 is more wisely invested for a place than for the win. (My results suggest maintaining these covering place interests on long-price selections. Check yours out, too. And if you don't keep results, start doing so right now.)

Hint 45: Be prepared to back more than one horse in a race

Sometimes you will form the opinion that more than one horse represents value for money in a race. The first thing you should do at this point is to review your analysis and confirm your opinions. Still convinced? Then be prepared to back both horses according to the level of value available. My only rider here is to ensure the combined odds are not too low. If you have obtained 5-1 about two horses in a race, for instance, you are effectively backing a 2-1 shot. This will suit many betting styles, although it is a little too conservative for my taste. I'd rather wait for another day.

Hint 46: Don't waste money on 'savers'

There will often be a niggling suspicion in your mind that a certain horse represents a big danger to your selection. It does not appear to represent value for money, but it keeps nagging away at you. To ease the pain of watching it come home in front, you decide to have a saver 'to keep it honest'. Eliminate these bets. If a horse is not value for money, you should never back it. There are no exceptions to this rule. Perhaps the nagging suspicion concerns your fancy.

Perhaps it is not as tempting proposition as it might appear. The unsettling presence of this saver horse can have its uses if it persuades you to review the chance of your original fancy and to cut down your bet if necessary.

Hint 47: Don't feel you must bet because it's Cheltenham or Royal Ascot or Goodwood

Some of the most difficult of all races to solve take place at the showpiece meetings, particularly the handicaps. Each race is extra competitive and the bookmakers, knowing they will be extra busy, do their homework even more thoroughly than usual - and that is extra thorough in the first place. The temptation is to have a bet, just to get involved. We all know the feeling - it's the Gold Cup and everybody's talking about the race. A couple of our favourite horses are running. We know the race looks hard to solve, but a small bet can't hurt...

Once again, our logic is faulty here. I can understand wanting an interest in a selling hurdle, or a poor handicap, which would have very little to recommend it as a spectacle without one, but why must we bet on the big races. Are not they interesting enough already? There is a related hint to be made on this point.

Hint 48: Remember - a loser avoided can seem like a winner

You have a couple of fancies for a day's racing, but cannot quite persuade yourself they represent value for money. The temptation here is to muddle around, to finesse a few pounds onto the first selection. Stop yourself. If both horses lose, you will be on good terms with yourself and perhaps feel virtuous - certainly in a better frame of mind - for the bets to come. Missing a loser is not as good a feeling as backing a winner - but there are worse sensations for the backer to experience, such as walking back from the betting shop knowing you have wasted the week's food money on a couple of horses you knew in your heart you should never be backing.

Summary:

The key to this section has been finding the appropriate type of bet for our selection(s). This is most unlikely to have been an extravagant multiple bet like the Yankee, but the Tote Jackpot and Placepot are possible bets of interest. Ante-post betting will also appeal, but we will probably be aiming to root out nearly all our each-way bets. We will be prepared to back more than one horse in a race on occasion, but will not be wasting money on savers. The motto 'If in doubt, stay out' applies in this section and we will be aiming to avoid backing too many losers.

stage **five**

staking

Hint 49: Get into position in plenty of time

A vital point this and again one insufficiently appreciated by the majority of punters. These days, if you wish to take the pick of the early prices in the credit offices, you will have to be prepared to ring on the dot of opening time - and even then it may be too late. (More on this thorny matter below.)

Sometimes the big firms 'guarantee' prices for a few minutes from opening time in the betting shops, so it is possible to strike a wager on your credit or debit account (albeit a trimmed down one) and to get the balance on at the same firm's shop at the bottom of the street. Very satisfying - although think of the time which could have been saved if they'd accepted the original bet.

For those planning to take a board price in a betting shop, I advise arriving 15 minutes before the off time. Spend the first few minutes writing out your betting slips. Remember, you may wish to strike more than one bet, depending on the price movements, so make sure you do not have to waste time scurrying around for a pen or a blank slip when a show comes through.

The weaker-willed amongst us should certainly take note of this advice. We can all recall the time we popped in to the betting shop with one selection in mind and were immediately distracted. Perhaps by a horse being nicely backed in a handicap at another course. Here it is being enthusiastically flagged by our in-house bingo caller - and we feel obliged to take a small interest, just to get us underway on the day, you understand. The horse runs a stinker (would it be too cynical to suggest that an agent of one of the big firms had initiated the gamble knowing the horse was a duffer?) and we were already off-balance, an unnecessary wound incurred before the day's major skirmish. If you ring to take a board price on a credit or debit account, call about 10 minutes before the off and ask for a first show.

If it is not available, request a commentary and await news. There is also the teletext betting services, but there is often a slight delay in transmitting information and this could cost dear if the market is volatile and prices are changing rapidly. If you are betting on-course, try to arrive in the betting ring just before the first prices are being posted. There can be a trade-off here with paddock watching, but it is my view that only experts benefit from a long observation of the horses as they mill around. Those of us who barely know one end of a horse from another often get the wrong signals. Those who wish to learn more on the subject might like to consult the chapter on paddock watching in Nick Mordin's excellent book *Betting For A Living*. When you have arrived at these points, you will be prepared to bet because you will also have made sure to...

Hint 50: Plan your stakes in advance

If there is one area which lets punters down more than a failure to appreciate the concept of value, it is inadequate staking. By inadequate staking, I do not mean having insufficient on (although this may be a factor) but inadequate in the sense of 'found wanting'. The problem is lack of preparation. Remember the tale at the start of the book, about the backer who missed out on the 7-1 for his nap selection. That is all of us at some time - perhaps at too many times. Just as we must calmly approach our form study and then our value analysis, so we must calmly plan our stakes.

It need hardly be said that the betting shop or ring is not the place to be undertaking this planning, for it is already too late. Let us imagine we are interested in horse X, whose minimum value price we have assessed at 6-1. Remember, this is the lowest price at which we will be prepared to take an interest. Hopefully we will be able to obtain bigger than 6-1 about X, perhaps even as much as 8-1 or 10-1. We need to plan a list of how much we plan to stake at each price. But first a hint, to drive this point home.

Hint 51: The bigger the price, the bigger the bet

We should have an idea in our mind about X's true chance in the race (perhaps

5-1). This is not a price which will fluctuate minute by minute as prices do in the ring, although a late change in the going or of jockey might well make a big difference to our assessment. Therefore it follows that the bigger the price we can obtain, the greater the value to be enjoyed. Preparing a list in advance will help us take advantage of this possible value. Depending on one's bank and staking plan, the list might look something like this.

Horse X: 2.45 Newmarket

Price available	Stake
5-1 or less	nil
6-1	£50
13-2	£80

Price available	Stake
7-1	£100
15-2	£120
8-1	£150
9-1	£175
10-1	£200

These will be the amounts we plan to stake at the given price. Perhaps, to take the ideal scenario, we scan the morning papers and see that 10-1 Horse X is readily available - or arrive at the betting ring to watch almost every bookmaker posting the same price. All seems clear. We step in and have an interest, staking £200 at the price and retire to the stands after a job well done. No problem it might appear but, believe me, so much can go wrong. Let us arm ourselves with some hints.

Hint 52: Don't prevaricate - if you see the price you want, take it

Value seldom lasts long. Maybe the price you want is only available in one or two places, perhaps a couple of early price lists, or with just the one board bookmaker on the back row. Get in there now! There is no time to get into a dither wondering whether the price will drift - or even to count out the necessary notes in your hand, if you are betting on-course. This should have been done already.

Worst of all...

Hint 53: Don't get greedy and wait for a bigger price if value is already available

Of course on occasions your horse will drift and it would have been possible to have obtained a bigger price. The chances are, however, that if you are onto a live horse, and one which represents value, the price will be shortening rather than lengthening. Occasionally there will be sound reasons to expect your horse to drift (maybe there is evidence that a number of other horses are strongly fancied or perhaps the over-round on the opening show is particularly large) and then you can be excused waiting - but make sure they are sound reasons and not the idle guesswork that is the result of greed.

To illustrate the dangers of prevarication let us return to Horse X and assume that 6-1 is available on the opening show. We wait, greedily hoping for some 7-1, but the market moves in the opposite direction and suddenly only 5-1 is available. We have missed the chance to strike a value bet and feel a mild sickness developing in the stomach. We know the 6-1 will not be returning. Before very long 4-1 will no doubt be showing. And the horse will win. We know that now. There was all the time in the world to strike a £300-50 and we missed out. Not a great bet but good enough. We have now reached one of the biggest danger points in betting.

Hint 54: Never chase imaginary winnings

This might seem to be an odd concept, but put yourself in the position of the punter who has just missed the 6-1. The amount he would/could have won is spinning around in his mind. He cannot bear not to take an interest, so he ends up calling for some 9-2. In fact, he strikes a bet of £270-60. Yes, he knows this is more than he planned to stake at the 6-1, but only a tenner for goodness sake.

And this way he wins almost as much as he would have done if he'd taken the 6-1. If it wins, he'll be happy. If it loses, well nothing much is lost. We've all done it. We've all been there. And, believe me, a good deal is lost in terms of damage to the spirit. After all, we have ended up backing a horse at a price which we have assessed as not representing value for money and this is about the worst crime a backer can commit. Perhaps we are now trying to convince ourselves that maybe 9-2 is value, after all, but it will not wash.

We could have stood firm. We could have told ourselves that we have missed the 6-1, which is a damn shame, but that nobody is perfect. In the hurly-burly of betting you cannot get everything right. The only thing to do is to leave the ring or the betting shop and to tough it out. Of course, we know the true chance of the horse winning the race shortened dramatically after we missed the price and that no doubt it will win. Most of them do. It is a nasty fact of life, dictated by the gambling gods, that if you miss a bet the horse wins. You have to learn to live with these nasty facts if you are to make anything of your betting.

Let us return to our punter, busy trying to justify his £60 at 9-2. He has told himself the tenner makes very little difference, and so it might seem if he is a man of means. But does his logic hold? Would he happily accept £10 being added to his grocery bill for no consideration at all? Of course not. This is probably the sort of punter who loses heavily on a bet he should never have struck and then moans about the price of a cup of tea in the bar.

This sort of reasoning simply will not do. The tenner does make a difference. Tot them all up if you're in any doubt and then work out what kind of holiday this type of bet has cost you over the years (say, a luxury month in the Bahamas?). The gambling gods are ruthless with this kind of bet. When the horse loses we console ourselves that it has effectively only cost a tenner (some consolation!). In fact, had we taken the 6-1 the horse might very well have won. But as soon as we stepped in for the 9-2, it became an outsider in the Foinavon mould.

Again, just consider your past results. These bets win about as often as the fluke National hero. The gambling gods ensure it. One more point by way of encouragement. Sometimes when you stand firm and refuse to chase imaginary winnings, the gambling gods do reward you by allowing the horse to lose. Only occasionally, admittedly, but it does happen. Suddenly, you are better off. It is almost like backing a winner. Your confidence returns, albeit by a roundabout route. And you have learned an important lesson, one which will save you hundreds or even thousands in the future.

Hint 55: Stay calm

After you have made your plans, make sure you stick to them. Be single-minded. As soon as the prices come through, act as planned. Dismiss all other thoughts from your mind. Don't even think about the later races. Betting shop managers are told to keep an eye out for the efficient, single-minded punter - the one who pops in for one bet, one winner, and is out of the shop before the stragglers are past the line. They have a little book on their desk in which they record your bets, and quite possibly a nickname which helps them recognise you. This will have been inspired by your appearance. (So if you are in the habit of betting in a luminous anorak, or maybe Bermuda shorts if the weather has turned, think again. Try blending into the background instead.)

If you start backing a few winners, head office will deem it necessary to become informed of your bets. This will involve an irksome delay as the already over-worked manager telephones for clearance. If you have requested a price, your bet will sometimes be knocked back. These are the facts of life in the betting shop, at least for the successful punter. Help yourself by getting on early in order that the manager has time to follow his instructions. And don't blame him or her for causing you anguish.

Blame the miserable accountants in the head offices who, it sometimes seems, are on a mission to drain betting of all the cut and thrust which is its essential appeal. Their spirit is encapsulated by the relentlessly dour Tom Kelly of BOLA, whose grim countenance suggests he was turned down for Sisyphus' old job pushing rocks up a mountain and had to settle for his current employment instead.

Then again, maybe BOLA have a cunning agenda beneath their endless public whingeing, because if there is a better incentive for wanting to bet with their miserable members than trying to impoverish them with a series of decisive coups, then I am unaware of it. Credit and debit card backers tend to suffer from the dreaded knock-back even more than betting shop punters, so must also be on their guard. It is even worth a hint to remind us.

Hint 56: Be prepared for the knock-back

Just as we have to watch ourselves when we miss a value price, they key here is to avoid being bounced into accepting a different bet than the one you intended to place when first picking up the receiver. The bookies' technique, when running scared of a particular horse, is to say, "You can have £25 on it at 6-1 and the rest at starting-price" - or words to this effect.

Never be tempted by these offers, which are an insult to the intelligence of their customers, who will know perfectly well that starting-price is almost certainly going to be shortened dramatically by the same bookies' own agents on the racecourse. (Odd how bookmakers claim they must reserve the right to knock back bets, yet throw their hands up in righteous anger when any suggestion is made to limit their activity on the racecourse.)

Another hint here, just to drum this one home.

Hint 57: Never bet 'with the needle'

My goodness it is tempting, after you are treated like dirt, to want to hammer in with the bet of a lifetime against these whingeing accountants who like to call themselves bookmakers. Don't. It's not worth it. Just walk away gracefully. You may have wondered why the big bookmakers feel it necessary to open their credit offices at least half an hour before their betting shops.

 Apart from allowing the convenient, if vacuous, excuse that the price must be shortened for credit customers in order to save some for the "regular clients in the betting shops", the reason is simple. A great deal of credit business comes from 'faces', namely shrewd and well-connected punters, plus some owners and trainers with runners on the day. The information passed on by these punters helps mark the bookmakers' cards before the betting shops open. Liabilities are clearly much more easily assessed if bets are first siphoned through one channel, namely a credit office, than the 2,000 or so shops run by a company like Ladbrokes.

This would appear to be nothing but sound business practice from our friends on the other side of the counter. In bookmaking, however, wherever there is a sound business practice there is nearly always a cynical one lurking in the shadows. In this instance, it is the bookmakers knocking back punters to paltry amounts, then using their information to save themselves many tens of thousands of pounds by manipulating the market on 'live' horses later in the afternoon.

There is a moral to be extracted from all this. If we are not to emigrate to America, Australia or Hong Kong and their more punter-friendly systems, we must attempt to understand as fully as possible how the bookmakers think and work in order to be in the best possible position to outwit them. If nothing else, if a multi-million pound conglomerate like Ladbrokes takes so much care in knocking back bets in order to boost its profits, then we must ensure that we take equal care of ourselves in order to protect our own welfare.

The big bookmakers have cultivated a strategy of freezing out shrewd punters for one very good reason - they know they can keep their shareholders happy by exploiting the bad habits of those who remain. It should grate as sharply as nails down a blackboard for any punter to give up his hard-earned cash to these faceless operations without the most tenacious of struggles.

So we return to our knocked-back bet. Of course we are not going to accept starting-price. Perhaps we shall feel it necessary politely to inform the telephonist that we do not wish to be insulted by such an offer, suggesting he or she informs the floor manager of our views. We put down the telephone. Now is the dangerous moment. We have succeeded in placing a much smaller bet than we wished, and perhaps expected to strike. We will inevitably feel frustrated, with a feeling of profits slipping like sand through our fingers. Smaller prices are probably being taken elsewhere. We feel we must act quickly. We find ourselves tapping out the number of another firm, quickly calculating how much we need on at the lesser price they are offering in order to win as much as we would have won if only the first bookmaker...

Here we need to stop and take a deep breath in order to recover our composure. If we are not careful we will find we have staked more than we originally planned at inferior prices. Being knocked back is frustrating, but it as much a part of the betting game as fallers, incompetent stewards, ill-judged race-riding and all those other events which seem to conspire against us.

Being detached helps us shrug off these unwelcome intrusions. Whatever happens, we must not fall into the John Major trap and allow ourselves to be dictated to by events. Try to stay in control. In the heat of the moment it can seem as if your entire betting future depends upon backing this one live horse. There will be others. Try to wait patiently for them. Hence...

Hint 58: Remember, there is always another day - don't feel you will always be missing something if you decide not to bet

I once read a strange and compelling book by Dr Frank Wallace entitled *The Advanced Concepts Of Poker*. It told the story of a successful card player, John Finn, and the techniques he used to win in his neighbourhood poker games. Finn's strategy was cleverly two-pronged. During the game, he ruthlessly exploited the weaknesses of the other players - whilst, both on and off the table, he attempted to keep the losers happy through the use of flattery and sympathy. In other words, his strategy bore a remarkable resemblance to that employed on a daily basis by our friends the bookmakers. They sweat day and night thinking of ways to separate the punter and his money, while constantly sweet-talking us about customer service.

Like the bookies, John Finn, was particularly hard on the winners. If he sensed a shrewd player had entered one of his games, he did everything in his power to drive him away, bar pointing a Colt 45 at his temple and showing him the door. Now, Dr Wallace's proposition, illustrated through the actions of Finn, was that anybody could win a million dollars off his neighbours at poker providing he employed the advanced concepts. It might take 20 years to win this money, but it could be done. And, boy, were there some cunning tips in this book.

John Finn, we were told, had himself made over $50,000 playing poker in the past year. Admittedly he'd had to sit in on over a hundred schools to make this money, but it was 1965. (I am indebted to David Spanier's wonderfully entertaining book *Total Poker* for this review, having lent my copy of *The Advanced Concepts* to a friend sometime in the early eighties, who never returned it.)

The book showed us how Finn had made this money. It had been hard work, believe me, not least the telephone calls to the losers, trying to tempt them in for one more game. They were, in a sense, his regular customers. As I have noted, John was particularly hard on the losers, making them pay dearly for their mistakes, however slight. I am still unsure of Dr Wallace's intentions but I am sure, like me, most readers ended up pitying Finn. Sure, we could admire him at a distance for his card-playing technique, but his life seemed curiously empty, devoid of any other interests. His whole existence revolved around winning money off his friends at poker. Gambling can do this to you - allow the obsessive side of your personality to come forward. Beware.

In the summer of 1989, I spent a week in Paris with a friend. We visited the galleries, museums, drank coffee, toured Left Bank bookshops for old copies of *L'Etranger*, the usual thing. We spent one afternoon in the Musee D'Orsay, wandering among the seemingly limitless array of sculptures and paintings. All I could think about was a horse who was due to run in a seller at Pontefract on the same afternoon. It so happened that I knew the horse was to be doing its best, although the form figures would neatly disguise its chance. A healthy return on one's money was to be expected.

The trouble is, how do you get on when you are hundreds of miles away on the fifth floor of a converted railway station, admiring the Van Goghs? By telephone, that's how. All morning I had told myself to forget about this horse, to leave it alone. I was on holiday for goodness sake, trying to forget it all. And hadn't Nashwan won the Derby only three weeks earlier? What need had I of another touch? I told myself there was always another day. (Although not for this horse, admittedly. It had been waiting a good six months for this type of contest. Everything was in its favour. Trip, ground, the uphill finish. It could be 14-1 - £3,000-£210, plus the tax, something like that.)

As we waited in the queue for Musee D'Orsay, I made sure to note the position of the pay-phones. Just in case, you understand. Within minutes I would surely be immersed in the beauties of some of the world's great art treasures, and all would be forgotten. My friend had no time for gambling. After Nashwan, he had advised me to pack it in because I would never have another winner like that. I had sort of agreed. But how do you stop? At the appointed race time, or some 15 minutes in advance, I could not resist any longer. I made an excuse about a call of nature and began to make for the ground floor. All the Manets and Monets, the Renoirs and Sisleys, were a blur of colour as I passed. Other patrons were elbowed aside. By chance, one of the telephones was free. It is easy to connect from Paris these days, just a bleep and you're through. I asked for the price of my horse. "I'm sorry," she said, "it ran in the last. Won at 8-1."

I'd got the time of the race wrong. I was half an hour out. I was tempted to ask about the opening price but I rang off. Imagined 14-1 into 10-1, finally 8-1. If I'd have been at home I could have spread this much around, maybe that much. Won so much more. Doubled up with another horse running tomorrow and which I'd been waiting a month to back. I went back upstairs.

"Did it win?" asked my friend, without raising his eyes from his catalogue.

"No," I replied.

Hint 59: Keep a sense of perspective

Let the above tale be a cautionary one for those who believe the life of a professional gambler or a professional racing writer/gambler is a bed of roses. There are worse ways to make a living, to be sure, but betting cannot be worth it if it is occupying almost every hour of your waking day. We must bet as a means to an end, not as an end in itself. We must enjoy our betting and enjoy its fruits, if we are lucky enough to find it bearing any. And we must be able to leave it behind. Even if we are betting, and enjoying it, we must still keep a sense of perspective, for events can swiftly overtake us.

Let us return to our bet on Horse X. Remember 6-1 is our minimum value price. We are in the betting shop and over comes the first show. It is precisely 6-1. We take an interest, as planned, proceeding to the counter and asking for £50 at the 6-1. Moments after the bet is accepted, Horse X drifts to 7-1. What do we do? We follow the next hint.

Hint 60: If your horse drifts, back it again

It is not uncommon for punters to get into a flap when a horse drifts. They begin to imagine all manner of horror stories, largely circulating around the prospect that their horse will not be doing its best. During our earlier form study we have already satisfied ourselves that we are on a trier, so there is no need for us to panic. If our selection hails from a gambling stable, no doubt we would prefer to witness a market move in the opposite direction (after our bet is on, of course), but such operations have been known to try to pull the wool over the bookies' eyes and win with an on-course drifter.

So we go in again for some of the 7-1, staking a further £30 at the price. We will now have a bet of £80 win at combined odds of a shade under 13-2. This is close to our original plan. Note that a further £50 at the 7-1 would leave us with a bet of £100 at 13-2 which is above our plan. If the horse drifts once more, say to 8-1, we back it again. Perhaps this advice is easier to give on paper than to put into effect in practice. (Come to think of it, this comment applies to all the advice in this book!) We may well be feeling a sense of regret at plunging in for the 6-1; perhaps we will be toying with the idea of chasing imaginary winnings and having more than we should at the 8-1 in order to try to win as much as we would have done if we had waited.

Hint 61: Never brood over what might have been

The central thesis of this book is that we plan in advance in order to be in control during the hurly-burly of the betting action. We are aiming to be able to keep our head when all around are losing theirs. Of course we will make bad decisions. Scores of them. We will pick out duff horses, make inaccurate assessments of their chance, take the wrong price at the wrong time. These decisions we must live with - and be able to quickly dismiss from our minds.

We can learn our lessons in the cold light of a post-mortem. The worst possible time to be changing one's mind about a bet or brooding about a past mistake is when the prices are posted and the runners are at the start for a race. Panic ensues, followed by bad decisions. A vicious spiral may develop if we are not in the midst of one already. Often, we will have to make the best of a bad job. On occasion, we will have to sit out and watch a horse we should have backed win. So be it.

Hint 62: Don't follow the steamer after it has steamed

Nobody likes to miss out on a good thing - and there is nothing worse than backing a loser in a race when everybody else has taken the early price about the winner, watched it shorten to half these odds and then saunter home. Equally, if everybody else is enthusiastic about a horse it can be catching. But then so can a cold. McCririck loves to get up a good head of steam about the day's best-backed horse. Hence the term 'steamer'. This steamer is often the headline horse in the Pricewise column in the *Racing Post*, or the lead selection from the *Sporting Life*'s new Beat The Book feature. By the time Big Mac is on the trail, the best prices have often gone. Sometimes the big firms promise they will hold them up for their regular customers in the shops, but you will be lucky to get more than a bus fare on at the top price.

Don't follow the herd and join in these gambles. If you have taken the best price all well and good (a certain satisfaction comes from watching Joe Public scratch around for some 3-1 when you are on at treble the price). If not, stay out. The value will nearly always have gone. Punters love to 'follow the money'. A horse only has to shorten a point or so in a betting shop, and some bright spark will come forth with the magic line, "They're backing it." Do not ask why "they" are backing it, ask why you are backing it. And if you are tending to back horses only after they are shortening in the betting, review your strategy. The winning punter is the one who gets in ahead of the crowd before everybody else is squashed in the rush.

Hint 63: Don't feel obliged to concentrate on the early-price races

This might seem perverse advice from one who launched a column to spot the value in these races, but so be it. We must move with the times. If all good things do not come to an end, then they are sure to lose their gloss. There is still some remarkable value to be picked up on the early-price races, but a number of factors have made life more difficult for the punter.

1) The bookmakers are even more on their guard than they used to be, knowing a rick can prove exceptionally costly. When one is made, the price often disappears with the morning mist.

2) Publicity. From being the province of the sharp and well-informed, early-price betting is now democratised. Everybody wants to get involved. Hence:

3) It is so much more difficult to get a serious bet on a fancied horse than it used to be. It is mighty frustrating to spend half an hour on the telephone in the morning, only to end up with half the bet you had hoped to obtain.

The blood pressure rises and you feel stressed before the day is underway. For this reason, I shall be cutting down on the time I spend studying the early-price races in the future - certainly those covered in the tipping columns in the trade press. Here is an example from my 1993 betting diary to illustrate the stresses and strains of early-price betting and the poor judgment they often induce in the backer.

Wednesday 28 April: am

I had developed a sneaking fancy for a horse called Hob Green in the 3.40 at Ascot today. Ladbrokes were out of line in posting 12-1. The big problem was I would be making my journey for an appointment at the BBC at precisely the time the credit betting lines opened for business.

There are not too many dilemmas worse than sweating on a crowded tube as the price evaporates for a horse you fancy. Amounts you might have won seem to tumble away before your eyes. But I had been making the journey to Shepherd's Bush often enough recently to know that there was a BT cardphone perfectly situated on the platform at Kensington High Street. Off there just before 9.30, make the call bang on opening time, then back onto the next train to change at Notting Hill Gate. In position in the cutting room by 10.00pm.

My timing on Wednesday could not have been better. The card was in the slot bang on 9.30. I was waiting for the connection when it occurred to me that I could not remember my account number with Ladbrokes. Nor was their card in my wallet. I put the phone down and stared at the station ceiling for inspiration. A pigeon called. 1CJ6? ICJ8? ICJ3? The number would not come. The time was now 9.35. The third District line train in as minutes drew into the platform. I scrambled onto it. Maybe I would have the number by Shepherd's Bush.

At 9.50, I was still clueless. I asked if they would take a bet with just my name and address. They agreed. Then they told me the price was now 10-1. I put a bet on anyway. I should not have done, but I did. These things happen. The horse met trouble in running and finished unplaced, which was no more than I deserved. Can early-price betting be worth it?

Hint 64: Beware of distractions

You have only five minutes in the betting shop before you must rush for an appointment - but the first show is not through yet. You promised you would be at your destination by a certain time but the race is delayed and you are now fretting about being late. You promised to do the shopping on the way home but are about to empty your wallet on a 5-1 shot. TS Elliott wrote about how we spent our lives being distracted from distraction by distraction.

Distractions are bad for judgment and bad for betting. If you have a busy day it will probably be best to abandon any ideas to bet. The biggest trap is to undertake a hasty analysis of a race and to get some kind of inkling about a horse. You have not the time to investigate its chance in greater detail, but you cannot get it out of your mind. You inquire about its price in the morning lists, just out of curiosity. It is a point or so longer than you were expecting. You have no time to ring around to see if another firm is offering better value and you place a bet at the first price offered. A familiar situation, no doubt, and one which should have the alarm bells ringing. I knew before I set out that April morning that I should forget the Hob Green bet, but my will was weak. I got no more than I deserved - just as the laws of betting dictate.

Summary:

We have realised this is one of the most important sections in the book - and will be making every effort to follow the advice and to get our staking in order. This will involve planning our stakes in advance and getting into position in good time, whether we are betting at home, on the racecourse or in the betting shop. If a price we have identified as value is available we shall take it, and not become greedy and wait for a bigger price to appear. If our horse does drift after our first bet we shall back it again at the bigger price. We will resolve to stay calm at all times and not chase imaginary winnings. We realise we will be knocked back on occasions but will never bet with the needle. We shall not brood over what might have been, nor feel we will always be missing something if we decide not to bet on a particular day, week or even month. We shall not be following the steamer after it has steamed and will realise there is more to betting life than the early-price races.

stage **six**

the result

Hint 65: Savour that adrenalin rush

When discussing the appeal of betting, the writer Jeffrey Bernard had it spot on. "When you've risked about 10 times more than you can afford and savoured the flow of adrenalin, it is hard to get excited about anything else." Every bet represents an artificially induced crisis. Life squeezed down to a moment of all or nothing. You oscillate from feelings of wild abandonment to icy fear and back again within an instant. You become feverish and tense. Your muscles threaten to seize up.

Sometimes the pins and needles pulse so strongly through your arms that it is impossible to raise your binoculars to watch the action. Such were my experiences when watching Nashwan in the 1989 2,000 Guineas. I tried to record my feelings in my diary, in an attempt to recapture the dizzying, even excruciating sensations I experienced that afternoon.

Saturday April 30, 1989

I left the paddock in ample time to take my place in the stands. Too much time, still too much time. I chose the press area, to avoid the crowds, and stood alone away from the conversation. I had muttered no more than a sentence or two since I had left my hotel over four hours ago. Friends knew to avoid me on a day such as this. The jauntiness of some nearby colleagues nearby began to grate. My nerves were shot. My skull felt wafer-thin, as if ready to shatter at any impact, at any more tension. When Nashwan cantered past the stands, the crowd hushed and sighed. He moves like a panther, the

Major said. I have felt a sense of awe on three occasions in racing - Troy's Derby, Shergar's Derby and the instant when Nashwan's handler let him go on Newmarket Heath and he rocked back under Willie Carson, then set off to post, a beast to its prey. A good mover's heels never seem to touch the turf. I knew from that one precious moment that he was utterly invincible.

The mile start was barely visible from the stands, shimmering in the bright afternoon haze. I let my eyes wander across the vast open spaces as I tried to get a hold on the moment, on my mood. The more you try to imagine yourself, the further away you seem. It was impossible to get a grip on things, to find any detachment. Two minutes to go. I felt sweaty again. And nauseous. And my aching eyes were lost in their sockets. The race was on. I tried lifting my binoculars to watch the horses, but my arms were leaden. I turned away and stared at the winning post until its red inner circle began to wander before my eyes. Get it over with. Just get it over with.

I raised the binoculars again with three furlongs to go, held them against the pins and needles, and saw that Nashwan was leading. Then I put them down again and began to scream, inwardly, deepening the threads of tension in my stomach. No words came out. I watched Nashwan home from the furlong-pole, just him, none of the others; just him, his blue silks, chestnut against green, Willie Carson, pumping.

He was leading, I could see that, though others were closing. I looked at the post again and he got there. First. He made it. Now I screamed, then punched the air - again and again and again. He got there. He did it. Somebody who didn't know me cheered and shook my hand. I let it go and punched the air again. And again. He did it. Pushed past the others to get to the unsaddling enclosure. He did it. Nashwan and the Major - 33-1. He did it!

A bet like Nashwan comes along once or twice a lifetime if you are lucky, but it is worth waiting for. In a sense, this book has been trying to show how it is possible to pave the way for a Nashwan, for these are not bets you can strike in lazy abandonment late on a Saturday afternoon. No doubt it is easy enough to stake more than you can afford at no more than a stroke and find the adrenalin coursing through your veins; many do, and quickly live to regret it.

The professionally-minded gambler is able to enjoy all the heady sensations of the gambling action, yet come out at the other end feeling cool and clear inside. It is as if he is intoxicated, yet totally clear-headed, able to lose control and yet keep control. Some have argued that to enter into the hard and lengthy calculations, the rigorous analysis which must form the backbone to a successful betting strategy, is to miss the essential appeal of the gamble. My belief, to the contrary, is that hard work frees one for the thrill. A gambler who has done his homework is able to make his mind a blank before a big race. No doubts, no petty niggles interrupt him.

Hint 66: Never bet if there is a chance you may come to regret it

I had staked a large amount on Nashwan - more than I might readily have wished to lose, yet I knew, beyond doubt, that I had done absolutely the right thing. This is the state of mind we should ideally find ourselves in after striking any bet. Everything should have been executed to plan - form study, value assessment and staking. These bets leave you with a glow of satisfaction inside before they have run. In this state you are truly free to relish the action, the charge and the adrenalin flow. My experience is that when you feel fully satisfied about a selection it nearly always runs well. Of course, had Nashwan lost, I would have been disappointed - indeed shattered for a time, yet there would have been no regrets. For I knew with utter certainty that I had done the right thing.

Hint 67: Don't try to 'get out of trouble; with indiscriminate bets

Hopefully, by sticking to a disciplined betting strategy, we will never find ourselves in trouble. Of course we will have bad losing days and long losing runs, but we will not feel a need to compensate with indiscriminate bets. After a disappointment, or at times when confidence is low, many punters feel a need for the reassurance of a winner. They will often find themselves backing short-priced favourites, or ill-considered, poor-value selections. This is an understandable fault, but one which must be resisted. Far better to leave the racecourse or betting shop immediately and find a quiet space where you can reflect calmly upon events.

Hint 68: Review each race in order to see what you have missed and to note pointers for the future

In reflecting calmly upon the result of a race, it will be worth taking another look at the winner's form in order to see what you missed or, more happily, to confirm your excellent judgement. Maybe you had failed to notice that the winner had a particularly good record at this time of the year, or over the course and distance. Perhaps it had gone well for today's jockey in the past? You will usually be able to find some line of form to explain a winner's performance, even that of an outsider.

Often you will not have taken this particular information into account when summing up the race. Undertaking a post-mortem can help train you to spot useful leads in the future. Equally, if you were on the winner, check that the race had gone to expectations. If you had foreseen your selection jumping out of the stalls and making all the running, then give yourself a pat on the back. But what about the horse you were lucky to hold off in the photograph. Had you underestimated its chance?

And make a note of other runners in the race, perhaps by watching the replay. I am not one who believes it is worth spending hours scouring the video in the hope of spotting a non-trier, or a horse who could have finished third instead of sixth with a better ride, but I do believe it is worth consulting a replay to confirm an opinion you might have developed when a race was being run. Disappointed though I was after Macs Maharanee was beaten in the Leicester race referred to earlier, I still made a mental note to look out for the winner, Blue Topaze, who had come with a spectacular late run to lead on the line.

The following month, encouraged by the way the Leicester form had worked out, I had a large bet on the filly to win a race at Newmarket and she was one of the unluckiest losers of the season - coming, as the *Timeform Perspective* put it "with a wet sail and just failing". This was the way my luck turned last season but the moral remains clear. Even when you are cursing your luck to the heavens, do try to find time to note the piece of information which could help turn things around for you in a week or so.

stage **seven**

winding down

Hint 69: Be a good loser

The Nashwans are rare. Most of the time we have to cope with losing and with disappointment. It is vital to be able to keep your equilibrium if you are to become a successful gambler. The famous American writer and punter Andrew Beyer tells the following tale in his book *The Winning Horseplayer*. The disqualification of a winner, Joanne's Choice, has cost Beyer $10,000. He has gone to the bar for a stiff drink and then squandered a few hundred dollars on the rest of the card.

"Two years earlier, at the same track, I had been unjustly disqualified out of $3,000, and was so frustrated and outraged by the injustice that I bashed a large hole through the wall of the press box. (It is still there with a frame around it and a sign that says 'Beyer's Hole'.) In the wake of the loss I was so upset that my handicapping and betting were adversely affected. I lost thousands of dollars more as a result. This was part of an all-too-familiar pattern. Throughout my life as a horseplayer, I had seen winning streaks turn into losing streaks overnight because a photo-finish, a disqualification or some other traumatic experience wrecked my equilibrium and caused me to alter methods with which I had been achieving success. It took me years even to perceive the nature of this boom-and-bust pattern, to realise that fretting over a set-back is the worst mistake a horseplayer can make ... tough losses are an inescapable part of the game, and the best way to deal with them is bemused detachment."

I have always been lucky in being able to quickly wipe a disappointment from my mind. If I am on a racecourse I will take myself into a quiet corner and review the events in my mind. Alternatively, I will leave the betting shop and sit on the nearest bench or have a cup of tea in a nearby cafe. If luck has been against me, I tell myself, it will even out in time. Of course this process is easier to undertake if you know the bet you struck was a good one. It is vital to cultivate this sense of bemused detachment. If not, like Beyer, you might find yourself betting 'on tilt' and quite probably undoing a good deal of hard work in the process, apart from damaging that most vital of attributes - confidence.

Hint 70: Be a good winner

By this, I do not mean ordering the champagne - although there may be times when this is appropriate. I am referring, once again, to keeping a sense of detachment. Too many punters enjoy a good win and then throw it all away with a series of ill-thought-out wagers later in the afternoon. I think it is just as important to take yourself into the quiet corner of the cafe and to congratulate yourself on a good winner. Try to identify those factors which led you to select the horse and resolve to look out for them again.

If you have no more bets to come, resolve also to spend the rest of the afternoon in a sense of serene, rather than bemused detachment. If there is more business to do, it may be worth playing up your stakes to capitalise on the mood. But keep everything within bounds. And don't believe that because you've backed one winner the game is suddenly cracked. Sadly, it isn't. But at least you are making the most of your good fortune. Maybe you will buy those drinks after all. But please, if you do...

Hint 71: Don't boast about winnings

I am afraid there will have been times when I have let myself down on this score. Perhaps we all have. Ego enhancement plays a large part in betting and the successful punter will inevitably have a high sense of self-belief. But this is no excuse to rattle on about your inspired judgment and how your winnings will be paying for a holiday here, or a new house there. Not only is it rank bad manners to boast in this manner, and thoroughly irritating for those who have just backed a loser, but the gambling gods are likely to ensure you end up with egg on your face by initiating a terrifying losing sequence on your very next bet.

stage **eight**

taking stock

Hint 72: Record all bets

There is no getting away from this one. Every bet must be recorded - from the mortgage-paying ante-post gamble down to those tiny 'just for fun' interests with which we like to while away the afternoon. If nothing else, this process will reveal that the 'just for fun' bet is actually not any fun at all at the end of the day, just costly and embarrassing. Some of the bets you have struck will certainly embarrass you, others will irritate and surprise. You will stare at your profit and loss sheet wondering, "Just what on earth possessed me to back that?" Other bets will give you great satisfaction.

There are few better feelings than returning at the end of the day to enter a winning bet onto your chart and to see the plus column extending inexorably into profit. Equally, it is damaging for the spirit to have to enter losses, but it must be done. Do not get into the habit of finding excuses, of telling yourself you had an off-day or a rush of blood. Equally, do not tell yourself that all your bets are recorded already on credit account statements or betting slips.

Every bet counts and there are few better disciplines than confirming as much by writing them down. If it hurts to record losers, try not to back them! I recommend recording not only the name of the horse, its finishing position and your stake, and the profit or loss on the race, but also your assessment of its minimum value price next to the price taken. This will give you an at-a-glance guide to the quality of your bets, but will also help you assess the accuracy of your price assessments.

For instance, if over the course of a season you backed 60 horses you identified as true 2-1 shots, around 20 of these horses should have won. If less than, say, 15 obliged and you cannot call upon a host of genuine hard luck stories to excuse the failures, then your assessment of their chance will have been too optimistic - 3-1 would have been a more accurate marker. Naturally, possessed of this information, your bets would have been radically different and far less costly. Recording bets allows for all manner of similar revelations into your betting and there is no excuse at all for not adopting the process. Hence:

Hint 73: Analyse these bets

I find it is useful to review each bet as you record it - and to do so again after a period of at least a month has elapsed. In betting, it is important to be able to trust your instincts and gut feelings but also to be able to reflect dispassionately upon events. At the time every winning bet might seem to be nothing more than you deserved, but the passing of time can allow a different light to be thrown upon it. I think it is vital to be able to draw the following distinction:

Hint 74: Distinguish between good bets and good results and vice-versa

To the uninitiated a good bet is a winner and that is the end of the matter. The skilled punter knows better. Sometimes we get out of jail and a bad selection obliges. Equally, our very best bets might have been losers. I am still inclined to think that my best-ever bet was beaten, namely Sweet Mover in the 1986 Extel Handicap.

The horse was trained by Dick Hern, who could boast a fine record in the race, winning it twice in the previous seven years and providing the second with Boldden 12 months earlier. Having shown some useful form in two starts as a juvenile, Sweet Mover made a belated reappearance in her second season, narrowly winning a small maiden at Chester. The form was nothing to write home about but she had been heavily backed to win the race and appeared capable of showing (quite possibly significant) improvement.

Knowing the Major's methods, I marked her down as a possible Extel candidate and one likely to get in with a low weight based on her paper form. This was an example where close following of a yard can add to a backer's confidence. When the four-day declarations came through, I accessed Sweet

Mover's name on the *Racing Post* computer. There she was, nestling towards the bottom of the handicap for the Extel.

A glow of satisfaction and anticipation came upon me and I had soon formed the conviction that Sweet Mover would just about win the race, despite the claims of a number of strong-looking rivals, including Luca Cumani's Celestial Storm. What is more, she was almost certain to be a long price given her modest-seeming form. This was before the days of Pricewise, but I told everybody who wanted to listen, and quite probably a number who did not, that they must be on Sweet Mover.

On the day, she was 20-1 and 16-1 in the morning betting and I struck the biggest bet of my life at these prices. Sometimes your confidence can drain after making such a bold move, but mine held. Indeed it seemed augmented and I twice went down to my nearest Ladbrokes to add to my bet. Sweet Mover started at 14-1 and was the winner everywhere but the line, where she was caught by the fast-finishing Chinoiserie, who was only picked up by the BBC cameraman in the shadow of the post. For a time the disappointment was shattering, despite the place proportion of my bet enabling me to recover my stakes.

I had another big bet later in the afternoon on stablemate Wassl Touch in the Alycidon Stakes, another of Hern's favourites, and a race in which I had landed a notable coup with Longboat in 1983. Despite having taken a substantial bet at the morning 12-1 and watched the price cut in half, I could summon no enthusiasm for the bet after Sweet Mover, and could barely raise myself from my chair to watch the race. Somewhat predictably, Wassl Touch ran a moderate race, finishing fifth of the eight runners, thus scuppering the bet and any hopes of drawing on a healthy place double with Sweet Mover.

Such flashpoints of excitement and disappointment can be exceptionally dangerous for the backer. It is hard to return to the ordinariness of everyday life after such a rollercoaster ride - and the temptation is to strike out at random with another big bet to keep the momentum going. And when you have already lost so much - be it cash or, as in this case, glory - another loser can seem to be neither here nor there.

Half an hour later, Hern had a two-year-old debutant running in the Chichester City Maiden Stakes. The horse's name was Merce Cunningham, a half-brother to the Irish Derby winner Caerleon. Hern has an exceptional record with his two-year-olds at Goodwood, particularly with the newcomers. I had backed a number of them to win tidy amounts. I crossed the editorial floor at the *Racing Post* to await the first show on the Extel screen, with feelings of anger and fear mixing with a far-away detachment. I did not want to back Merce Cunningham, yet it would have been the last straw to watch the horse open at 7-2, be supported into 9-4 and win in a canter. The opening price was 7-4, hinting at how strongly he was fancied, yet too short to attract interest even in my current state. I managed to drag myself away from the screen.

Silly thoughts are apt to run through your mind at such times - like, shall I back the horse to get back my losses on the day? Why these bets can have an appeal at the end of the day which they would not have had at the beginning is something of a mystery, but they do. I resisted. Merce Cunningham was supported into 11-8, but could finish only third.

If I recall correctly, I lost my appetite for betting for the best part of a week after Sweet Mover, which was something of a blessing in disguise, for it is often tempting to try to repeat the dose after such a bet, to find another such horse on which to go to town. Objectivity is lost. In fact, this may be worth a hint in its own right.

Hint 75: Avoid unnecessary repetition of bets

I used to open the batting for my school cricket team. I was no Boycott, to put it mildly, but could execute the occasional immaculate cover drive. My problem was, one such shot and I thought I was Boycott. At the very least I wanted to retain the sweet glow of surprised satisfaction which comes from a perfectly-timed shot to the boundary. Indiscriminate shots would follow and I would very soon be on my way back to the pavilion, cursing my impatience.

Backers are much the same. One winner (or perhaps one big near-miss like Sweet Mover) and we are anxious for more of the same. Let us bring in Geoff Boycott again. Our three D's for successful betting - DETACHMENT, DISCIPLINE and DEDICATION - were three qualities Boycott could boast, allied to a supreme technique and extraordinary powers of concentration. One of his most telling observations about batting was that each ball should be treated on its merits, regardless of what had gone before. You put the memories of the last ball out of your mind and concentrated only on the next, whether you had just hit a four, a streaky single, or been dropped by the wicket-keeper.

The same point applies to horse-race betting, indeed to all forms of gambling. You must be able to make your mind a blank between betting opportunities in order that one bet does not affect the next and a vicious spiral develop. Recording and analysing bets helps you identify when you have fallen victim to this process and to recognise when you are in danger of doing so again in the future. This point bears emphasising. There are three essential stages to the gambling process, whether you are backing horses or numbers on a roulette wheel.

1)   Decision making (i.e. selection and staking)
2)   Action
3)   Wind down

The backer must aim to keep all three discreet - i.e. not to allow one to run into the next. Hence the need to cultivate detachment. You should plan your selection calmly in your mind, then place your bets (the decision making). When the race is on, you should relish the excitement and adrenalin flow (the action). And when the race is over, you should quickly take stock of events, come to terms with them and move on (the wind down).

Think of the golfer. He lines up his shot to the green, assessing the lie of the land, the wind, flag position and any other relevant factors. Then he selects the appropriate club (the decision making). He plays his shot (the action). And assesses the results, before moving onto the next shot (the wind down.) The next shot may be a vital chip or putt. If he is still fretting with himself over his selection of club for the last shot, or brooding over the trajectory of his backswing, or recalling a bad putt he made three holes ago, he is in trouble. He has lost his detachment.

Hence the problems some unfortunate golfers get with the 'yips'. They bend down over a putt and all manner of crazy and random thoughts begin to cascade across their minds, not least how much money a miss might cost. They simply cannot clear their minds in order to plan and execute the putt. They begin to sense, even know, they are going to miss. The doubts communicate themselves to the body and all manner of involuntary shakings and spasms affect the putting stroke.

And they do miss. The yips can become so over-powering some golfers cannot bear even to walk onto a green, let alone bend down over a putt on which a championship could swing. I know from my own experience how mental attitudes can affect one's game. Sometimes you stride up to a putt, analyse the line and confidently stroke it into the middle of the hole. At another time the identical putt can seem a million miles away, the hole seeming to shrink before your eyes. Perhaps more than any other this hint is easier said than done, but here it is...

Hint 76: Don't beat yourself

Once you have acquired a good technique for winner-finding and value assessment, betting is nearly all in the mind. The aim, it might almost seem, is to be able to free yourself to win, to clear away all the fog, the doubts and the fears which have clogged up our betting for so long. Most punters seem to be fighting a running battle with themselves. They seldom feel ordered and settled, nor harmonious inside. This book aims to clear the doubts and fears and to provide for the positive states of mind which are essential to winning gambling. Here are some more tips to aid this process, each facilitated through the essential bet recording/analysing process.

Hint 77: Don't make the same mistakes over and over again

This may be over-critical, but I get the impression that a large number of punters never learn from their mistakes. They just keep on backing the same hopeless horses in the same hopeless manner and they keep on losing. Most of us learn some of the time, but not enough. Of course it is damaging to the self-esteem to have to acknowledge you have just spent the entire afternoon betting like a beginner, but so be it. A backer without the faculty for intense self-criticism is doomed to failure.

Hint 78: Don't fret about bad luck

It is a feature of the betting process that if you want an excuse to explain your failings there will always be one to hand. Mostly, they can be summed up in four words, perhaps the most costly four words in betting - "Luck was against me." We all have our stories. The day Henry Cecil sent out five winners and you backed his only loser - the horse who was 20 lengths clear at the last and jumped it perfectly, only to lose its balance when landing in a divot; the day the Northern Line came to a halt between Waterloo and Embankment and you missed a 16-1 winner during the delay; the fact that you did 20 each-way doubles in the last season and backed fourteen winners, but never two together; the injuries to your ante-post selections; the bad rides; even the day when you were in a hurry to compile your Placepot and wrote number five instead of six - and six came up and...

The list is endless. Like fishermen, we love to talk about the one that got away. And tend to remember them too, ahead of the streaky winners. After all, if a rival falls at the last and presents the race to your horse it was no more than you deserved wasn't it? It is one of the few certainties in betting that if you approached a hundred punters on the racecourse or in the betting shop and asked them whether, on balance, they tended to be unlucky or lucky in betting there would be a big majority in the former camp.

Let it be emphasised here and now that luck is such a small part of the betting process that it hardly matters at all. Got that? Luck hardly comes into it. Of course there are fluctuations, often of a wild and unpredictable nature, but they tend to even out over time. If in doubt, study your betting results. Still not sure? Then consider the following examples.

Say I choose to back my favourite number at roulette. A single number pays 35-1. My first bet loses. On the second, the ball slows, appears to be settling in my groove, but bounces out at the last possible moment into the adjoining number. Am I unlucky? Alternatively, I back my favourite number in a horse race, without any study of the form. My horse starts at 10-1 and is 25 lengths clear when falling at the final hurdle. Bad luck? The answer, effectively, must be no. There was certainly an element of ill-fortune in the chosen betting process but, in truth, I brought this bad luck upon myself, I invited it by the folly of my actions. In the long run, it is statistically impossible to win at roulette by backing a single number (or indeed any other bet on the table) or by choosing a horse at random.

Now this might appear to be a serious, overly-didactic approach. The losing gambler might argue that he goes to the roulette wheel or the horse race for some fun, for a slice of action, so why should he get worked up over this impossible-to-win argument? Surely life is too short? And what about the player whose number just came up, who collected at 35-1 and is now skipping to the champagne bar? Are we trying to argue he brought his (good) luck upon himself? It is perfectly reasonable behaviour to gamble for fun and not to get worked up about the odds and chances, the impossible-to-win argument. Many people do, on Bingo for instance. But it is contradictory to want to gamble for fun, and not to have to worry about odds and chances, then to moan about the result when it goes against you. The ill-luck in our examples concerned the result. Those wanting their fun got it. The wheel span and the horses ran.

Those moaning about their bad luck clearly wanted more. They wanted fun and a good result, but their actions opposed their wishes because they made a bet which was bound to lose in the long run. Luck is like time, it flows. We break it down into artificial segments (e.g. minutes, results) for our own convenience and understanding. It could be argued that the gambler in our above example enjoyed many moments of good luck during his horse bet because it was in the lead nearly all the way before falling. It could have come down at the first hurdle. But those who start moaning about the result allow the bad luck of falling to override any fun they might have had from the bet. They impose this meaning on the event. They could have shrugged their shoulders and walked away. Now what of the winner, the gambler whose number has just come up? Surely he was lucky to win? In that one, artificially isolated moment, so it might appear.

But maybe he had struck 50 losing bets on this number earlier in the evening or over the years. Maybe his overall gambling record is worse than everybody else in the casino. Without extra knowledge, to describe this winning gambler as lucky is equivalent to suggesting I am a careless person if I trip over a stick in the street. In the moment, so it might appear, but it is another matter to begin to generalise about me from this one piece of evidence.

Alternatively, our winning gambler may have come into the casino in a light-hearted frame of mind, prepared to have a few bets and go home with a smile win, lose or draw. He knew that roulette is a game of chance so he decided to back a lucky number rather than have a blind guess. Once his number came up, he retired to the bar to celebrate. Were this gambler's bet to have bounced out of its groove at the last moment, he would no doubt have treated it as one of those things and walked away as if nothing had happened. Cultivating, as we are, a spirit of detachment we too should be able to walk away from momentary bad luck, trusting it will even out in the long run.

We are in the Gary Player mould, believing that the more we practice the luckier we will get. If you continually take 2-1 about a genuine even-money shot (indeed if you continually take value at whatever position on the scale), you will - all other things being equal - be a winner in the long run. Misfortune will occur along the way. But then the wise man, like the wise punter, considers misfortune and arms himself against it in advance.

Hint 79: Stake consistently

This is among the most vital hints in the book, perhaps the most vital hint. Let us return to the punter in our cautionary tale, able to take the 2-1 about the genuine even-money shot. That is, 2-1 about heads occurring on the toss of a coin. He is given 20 plays. Here is the sequence of results.

T T H T T H H T T T T H H H T H H H T T

Our punter could have been luckier, for there were eleven tails and only nine heads and he was backing heads. But, betting at a level £10 stake, he still emerges with a profit of £70. Let us now assume he shuns the consistent, level-stake approach, finding it too tedious. He decides to bet according to whim, and mood. The winning sequence is exactly the same. But study his stakes on the right, and his thought patterns.

T £10 (a steady start), T £10, H £10, T £10 (still keeping things steady), T £10, H £10, H £10, T £20 (had a good feeling after two wins so upped the stakes), T £20 (kept going expecting luck to even itself out), T £10 (felt like increasing stake, but adjusted at the last moment), T £20 (pleased at last decision so upped stake), H £10 (didn't work so back to normal), H £10 (lacked confidence after just the one win), H £20 (feeling better now), T £30 (even better - damn!), H £10 (don't push things), H £20 (not much time left so began pushing things), H £30 (and again), T £40 (and again - damn!), T £80 (last stake so tried to go for broke, staking all winnings).

Betting in this manner, our punter draws level, a dismal effort considering how much the odds were in his favour. It is my guess that our staking is closer to that of the punter in the second example than that of the first. Remember the time you went to a race meeting and backed the first winner. You upped your stakes on the next two bets and they both lost. Back to normal for the fourth bet, which won. By far the biggest bet in the last race, which lost.

Or the time you had planned a nap selection on the third race, but lost on the first two races. Feeling gloomy, you dropped your planned stake on the nap, which won. Frustrated at calculating how much you should have won if only you had kept your head, you staked far too much on a guess in the last, which lost. There is no excuse for having £50 on selection A one day and only £10 on the identical selection the next. Sod's Law, of course, dictates the under-staked selection obliges and the other is beaten.

I am ashamed to say that my betting has been plagued by inconsistent staking, and that I have suffered as a result, not just financially, but in terms of frustration and disappointment. In my early years, I would play up my stakes after a big win, usually indiscriminately. After a time, it became clear that I would nearly always blow my hard-won gains within six weeks of a big win.

This 'six-week factor' became so ingrained in my thinking that I would walk home from the betting shop or return from the racecourse after a good day telling myself, "It's a good win but it will be gone by so-and-so." More often than not, so it proved. Again, the emphasis is on detachment, upon treating each bet on its merits. By all means increase your stakes within sensible proportions after a good win but avoid indiscriminate betting. Some punters prefer to bet to level-stakes, or alternatively to back each selection to win an identical amount of money. Given that the proportion of value obtained on each selection inevitably differs (there is a world of difference between obtaining 6-1 about a genuine 5-1 shot and 10-1 about the same horse), I have never favoured level-stakes betting, although it will suit those punters who tend to back within a narrow price range.

Try totting up your total stakes on, say, the last six months' betting. Divide this figure by the number of selections. Taking the resulting amount as a theoretical level-stake, tot up how you would have fared backing to this method. If betting to level-stakes would have been significantly more profitable, you might consider switching to this method.

Another staking method involves backing each selection to win an identical amount of money. This approach is open to the same objections to those raised above, but could suit those who tend to back in a wider price range. Again, test out your past betting results. Whatever your views on the above staking methods, I believe it is good advice to:

Hint 80: Back every selection to win a minimum pre-set amount

This can act as a reminder to avoid those small, yet costly, 'just for fun' bets. Indeed, if you set your minimum amount relatively high, as I believe you should, it will help instill greater discipline into your staking. If you are not happy at the prospect of backing a horse to win your minimum amount, leave it alone, don't compensate with a lower bet.

Hint 81: Be prepared to encounter losing runs

Losing runs are the bane of every backer and can undo the good work of weeks, months, even years, especially if you are unprepared for them. I have always been prone to long losing runs, no doubt because I have tended to back the more adventurous selections. Mind you, my first 17 bets in a casino were losers, placed on the 25-36 segment. The chance of this happening was a shade over 780-1. It was a numbing and costly experience.

Of course, I had no business being in a casino as a value-oriented punter, but one sometimes has to see how the other half lives (or perishes). I watched the first five losing spins with a feeling of amused detachment, telling myself that luck would soon change. By the end of the second five, I could feel the muscles tightening at the back of my neck and my knees beginning to tremble. A friend brought over a complimentary cup of coffee to where I was standing. The two chairs around the table were both taken. I had a dreadful vision of spilling the scalding liquid onto the immaculate green baize. I trusted my voice was betraying no emotion.

The English gambler is famed for his composure under fire, for maintaining poise and dignity as he fritters away a fortune. There was a suggestion to move tables or to switch casinos, but you would have needed five strong men and one of those jackets with arms at the rear to get me away from that table. It had to be seen through. I was not budging until my number had come up, until the run had been ended. No gambler can bear to leave such a sequence hanging in the air.

Nagging questions began to buzz through my mind. Why did I know, with something approaching certainty, that if I switched my bets to a lower group of numbers the abandoned ones would start to come up, but if I stuck it out, petulantly, stubbornly, on the original choices I would continue to be insulted in this manner? Why, in the space of just 15 spins, had number 5 come up three times, enabling an immaculate Arab gentlemen to reel in a pile of chips so large he would have injured himself if he jumped off them? And number 8 twice? On consecutive spins? Why did I feel something approaching anger for the roulette ball as it tumbled and bounced, inevitably, into the wrong hole?

Finally, on the 18th spin, number 35 obliged. The croupier awarded me two winning chips in the same cool, efficient manner she had adopted when dragging in the 17 losers. I considered letting the winners ride, in the manner of the true casino gambler, then pocketed them and told my friends I wished to leave. Roulette is a transfixing game and I do not recommend it. As Einstein once commented: "No one can win at roulette unless he steals money from the table when the croupier isn't looking."

But the losing run I have just recalled, condensed as it was into no more than half an hour, does at least provide an illustration of the emotions which will wash over the unfortunate horse race backer, whose losing run might extend into weeks, even months. There is the tension, the feeling that things are slipping away, like sand through your fingers. The irrational speculation. The desire to hit out, to change your plans in order to get it over with. The stubbornness. The lack of trust in your own decision making. The cursing and fuming. The loss of confidence. The anger. More loss of confidence. The feeling that you no longer care, for what is another loser after so many? The mood swings, from laughter to despair. My worst run on the horses came in 1990 when I backed 49 losers on the trot. I later described the sequence in an article in *Odds On* magazine and a reader approached me at the races and said he did not believe me, that I had made the figure up for dramatic effect. I told him I only wished it were true. I have only once been genuinely scared about my betting and it was at the end of this sequence.

I had always toughed out past losing runs, trying to maintain my style and waiting for the tide to turn. This sequence tested that brave and foolhardy notion to the limit. The 49th loser was a horse called Vintage in the Bessborough Handicap at Royal Ascot.

The horse, you will perhaps not be surprised to learn, was trained by Dick Hern. I'd had him earmarked for this race for nearly a month, ever since a promising reappearance run at Goodwood. Hern liked to lay one out for the Bessborough and the stable's Vouchsafe had been first past the post in 1986 and 1988, although he was expensively disqualified on the former occasion. The trip and ground were ideal for Vintage, a four-time winner the previous season, and I was fully confident he would go close, despite the inevitable caution and pessimism induced by the losing run.

I made the bold and no doubt reckless decision to back him to recover the entire losses from the winning sequence in one fell swoop. The morning price was a highly-attractive 14-1, five points bigger than starting-price. Even as I walked to the betting shop I was still convinced that Vintage would just about win, although the tension was overwhelming. I kept telling myself that when I have a strong intuition about a horse winning, it nearly always does. Vintage ran a deplorable race, finishing 11th of the 17 runners, having never shown with a chance.

I left the betting shop and took a train into London feeling a genuine sense of shock, akin to that which comes after witnessing a traffic accident. Later, when the fog had cleared from my mind, I made a resolution not to bet until the Glorious Goodwood Meeting. I kept that resolution and my first bet back was a 7-1 winner. The serious backer cannot go for coaching in the manner of a sportsman who finds himself out of form, but there are steps you can take to limit the damage.

1) Take a breather. How I realise the benefit of this advice following the Vintage run.

2) Check your bets over and over again, review and criticise them. This can

enable you to feel you have a grip on your position. A tough losing run might not seem quite so bad once the losses have been totted up and compared to a winning period from earlier in the year - or after it has been noted how just one or two perhaps unlucky losers would have turned the sequence around had they obliged. (Equally, it is sensible to note down and review your winners during a profitable run, to avoid exaggerating your success.)

3) Stick to trusted methods. Don't play unnecessarily safe by picking out short-priced favourites simply to end the run. Equally, do not start backing outsiders in the hope of getting it all back in one hit.

4) And don't keep cursing your luck. Easier said than done - perhaps impossible in such a situation - but it is precisely when in the midst of a losing run that the old chestnut about negative thoughts always being punished comes into play. I am convinced there are waves and forces emanating from our minds which can make luck run for us, good and bad. Think of the notion of the 'rub of the green', particularly in a game like snooker. There is no doubt that when you are in the groove the balls roll into pockets when otherwise they would stay out. And vice versa.

When you cannot pot a ball all the flukes seem to go against you. But this is not to exaggerate this phenomenon. The problem is that we tend to impose extra meaning upon negative flukes, say by turning to our partner after one such incident to emphasise the global injustice of it all. The problem is that we let bad luck get to us. We become tense, agitated and unfocused - and hence we lose. This is no more than a common sense observation, for you cannot succeed at anything if you are in such a state.

And we can all recall those times when the more we tried to solve a puzzle or complete a job, the more we strained, the further away from success we seemed. It all comes down to detachment again. This is a state of mind we must cultivate over our betting in order that we are not to be swept along like sand when the inevitable bad losing run occurs.

Hint 82: Try to reduce the number of bets you strike

A best way to avoid a long losing run is to back fewer selections! We are nearly all guilty of having too many bets. Like a good gardener or wine grower we must prune. Expel those careless last-second wagers, the uncertain savers, and optimistic doubles and forecasts. Indeed...

Hint 83: Make sure you care about every bet

There have been occasions when I have missed the price about a horse and taken a small (indeed, sometimes not so small) interest at inferior odds, just to keep the horse 'honest'. Later in the day, and sometimes during the race itself, I might find myself calculating how much I would have won had I got the full intended bet on. These thoughts will sometimes have been sufficient to induce a desire that the horse loses, despite the fact there would be healthy winnings to come from the compensation bet.

This ridiculous behaviour inevitably destroys any enjoyment one might get from the bet, which should be among the first candidates for pruning. Indeed, I believe you should apply the following imaginary test to all your bets - namely, should you be deprived of this bet would you be inclined to struggle, even fight, to recover it? Would you feel deprived of something important to you, like a painter who finds a work missing from his studio?

Bets may not be works of art, but they are often nurtured, worried over and cared about. Try to make sure every bet you strike can pass this test. Be ruthless. Don't let the winners off the hook. You will be surprised at just how many unnecessary wagers you have been striking. Out of 85 from my 1993 summer, only three survived this test (and none of the winners).

Hint 84: Be prepared for the unexpected

As you will probably know, the longer you bet, the more likely it is that the strange and unexpected will occur. The most amazing story I have heard concerns Derek McGovern, the Sports Editor at the *Racing Post* and the man who has done more than any other journalist to highlight the tremendous opportunities available to the punter in his field.

Some four years ago, Derek had a dream that an unknown Canadian, Bob Chaperon, would win snooker's 1990 British Open. He was due to write a tipping piece the day after the dream, but declined to pass on his insight to his readers, although he informed his colleagues on the sport's desk. Chaperon's odds were 150-1.

Two weeks later, Derek watched in stunned silence as the Canadian beat Alex Higgins in a relatively one-sided final. I am afraid I have never dreamed a winner, although I did visualise the finish of the 1990 Derby to an uncanny degree of accuracy, witnessing a horse called Blue Stag coming from behind to claim second place from Elmaamul. This indeed happened - but the identity of the winner, regrettably, was not disclosed to me.

I have already described Jung's interest in the occult, but it is a little known fact that his great rival, Freud, took an interest in the para-normal, even if he was disposed to keep it secret. He was particularly interested in numerology, the belief that there are hidden harmonies in groups of random-seeming numbers (such a belief has been the downfall of many a roulette and Placepot backer). "I am not one of those who dismiss the study of so-called occult psychic phenomena as unscientific, discreditable or even dangerous.

If I were at the beginning rather than at the end of a scientific career, as I am today, I might possibly choose just this field of research, in spite of all the difficulties," he once commented. Maybe there will soon be an 0898 telephone service specialising in dreamed winners. Such is the credulity of punters that it could be big business indeed. Unfortunately, there is a law in the occult world which dictates you cannot profit financially from your psychic powers - not that this will have been any consolation to Derek McGovern.

Summary:

We will savour betting's adrenalin rush but not be lured into striking indiscriminate bets which we may come to regret. We will be both a good winner and a good loser. We will record all our bets, even the irritating ones. These bets will be heavily scrutinised. We will avoid making the same mistakes over and over again, and be able to distinguish a good bet from one which happened to win - and vice versa. We will not fret over bad luck, nor beat ourselves by becoming pray to distractions. We will be prepared to encounter the losing run and not be thrown off course when one occurs. We will be trying to reduce the number of bets we strike and will care about each one. We will be prepared for the unexpected.

stage **nine**

betting for a living

I know from my postbag that the idea of betting for a living or turning professional holds a great appeal for many readers. There are clearly a number among you who have confidence in your ability to make a profit from your betting and who want to know what extra is involved in betting full-time. The curiosity is understandable. Unlike most jobs, where you are at the beck and call of others, the professional gambler manages his or her own affairs. He is a free agent, able to make decisions on his own behalf unfettered by outside interference, and one who stands or falls on the outcome of those decisions.

The world of racing and betting can also seem a good deal more colourful than other jobs and professions. However, the hard truth is that if we define a professional punter as one who makes his living solely from horse racing and related forms of gambling, there are no more than a handful operating in Britain. There are a number who combine betting with running tipping and other advisory services, and a good deal more semi-professionals, who supplement their income through betting.

These facts should make it clear that it is exceptionally difficult to establish yourself as a professional punter in Britain. The betting culture in Britain is wholly against the professional - unlike, say, America or Hong Kong, where the on-course Tote pools are strong enough to encourage the shrewd and informed to play in amounts big enough to make it worth their while. A Tote system seldom, if ever, refuses a bet, but you cannot stake £100 in most pools in this country without ruining the dividend.

The professional punter is in essence a businessman and it is not surprising that he should wish to diversify into other, safer areas such as tipping (as successful backers such as Clive Holt of *Fineform* and Patrick Veitch, 'The Professional', have done). Cynics with their "If they were that good they would have retired to the Bahamas" lines should ask themselves if they would be prepared to put all their eggs in the fragile gambling basket. Nearly all professional and semi-professional gamblers rely to some part upon their information networks. Some, like Veitch, see a parallel with the City, not just in describing their bets as investments, but also in how rumours and gossip can affect the market. Veitch's preferred commodity is information on unraced two-year-olds.

Nobody doubts the lure of being 'in the know'. This would explain the surfeit of premium rate tipping services and telephone advice lines. The tipsters on Channel 4's Teletext service certainly appear to be onto something - everyday, it seems, they know of the "best bet of the year" or a horse who "cannot lose". Some of these tipsters do offer a fine service, including the Winning Line team, Clive Holt, Veitch and the excellent Nick Mordin. Many others have hopped onto the gravy train, knowing there are enough punters out there willing to pay good money to hang on the end of a telephone line, awaiting an endless stream of ill-informed and often inarticulate clap-trap.

Mind you, the rip-off merchants often claim a moral basis for their actions. The line is that there is certain proportion of mugs out there who are going to throw away their money whatever happens and it is better they should be helping a tipster on his way than the real villains. I am not sure this reasoning would stand up in an ethics class, but never let it be said these men cannot spin a decent yarn. For those of us without a telephone book of inside sources, there is still hope. Indeed, the real satisfaction from betting comes from having a substantial wager on a horse you have picked out yourself, against the advice of almost everybody else, and seen waltz home at what used to be referred to as a working man's price.

I discovered during my summer of betting that I had no aspirations to become a professional - partly because I do not have the ideal temperament, but mostly because I would prefer to spend my time on other things, like debating ethical dilemmas in philosophy classes. It is impossible to become a successful professional without devoting endless hours to the study of form and the search for value. And there is the question of experience. One greatly respected professional stated it took him nearly 20 years to truly make the game pay. With this in mind, I would be dishonest to claim this is a book which will help turn the reader into a professional punter overnight, or even in so many years' time. But the word 'professional" is nevertheless a useful one for our purposes, stressing as it does notions of organisation, skill and dedication. Rather than aiming to become a professional punter, we should be seeking to punt professionally - that is, to bet on an organised, disciplined and carefully planned basis, within our chosen strategy.

Punting professionally does not necessarily involve planning to win large amounts, the 'ticket to the Bahamas' of our earlier cynic. Each punter should set achievable financial goals and build their strategy around these targets. If, for instance, you have just retired and would like to supplement your pension with a little extra income from betting, just enough for the occasional weekend away perhaps, or presents for those close to you, then set your targets accordingly. Nobody can or should be trying to dictate to you, the punter, how you should be betting. We are in this business to try to escape from the petty tyrannies of our everyday lives. So this is our goal - to bet professionally on the terms we set for ourselves.

Hint 85: Make detailed plans

It is usually a mistake to hurry into any decision in life, but it would be folly of the highest order to set out to make your living from betting without giving the matter the most intensive consideration. Firstly, there is the matter of your betting bank. It is one thing to set aside money for recreational betting and quite another to do so knowing your livelihood depends upon it. Betting takes on a totally different complexion when your financial future is at stake. All manner of tensions begin to creep in. So ask yourself: does the prospect of betting for a living scare me more than excite me? If your answer is in the affirmative, then the option is probably not for you. No punter can expect to make a reliable profit if he is beset by fears, doubts and tensions. (Of course you do not have to be betting for a living to be subject to these emotions.)

Then take a long hard look at your finances. How much have you to put aside for your betting bank and how much do you need to earn in a year in order to get by? Study your past betting results, taking in at least the last five years. (If you have not kept such results, it is almost certainly premature to be considering betting for a living.) Calculate your average rate of profit on turnover, year-on-year. I suggest you should have been in the black on at least four of the last five years. Any rate of profit over 10 per cent, after tax, is good going and suggests you have been on top of the game. Anything less and you might want to consider brushing up your technique before taking matters any further. The pruning exercise referred to in Hint 83 will be worth undertaking. Strip out the unnecessary bets and then assess your figures again. Take care not to fall into the trap of assuming all the winners were good bets - indeed be especially ruthless with the winners.

The average annual income in Britain is said to be around £17,000. Therefore, based on a profit margin of 10 per cent, you would need to stake £170,000 per annum, excluding tax and expenses, in order to earn this amount. That is more than £3,200 per week, or over £500 per day. Once again, do these amounts frighten you? (It is worth noting that, betting purely off-course, your net rate of tax here would be 50 per cent.) Then there are expenses to be taken into consideration. These can mount up unawares and it is vital to undertake advance planning.

Ideally, you should set aside another bank purely for expenses. These will certainly include newspapers, form books and telephone charges, quite probably travel and admission costs to the racecourse, food, drink, maybe hotels and possibly an SIS link. There will also be the matter of your status for tax purposes and other related financial matters. See your accountant if in any doubt.

Hint 86: Be realistic

Ask yourself whether you can honestly foresee yourself sustaining the necessary level of betting and a constant stream of expenses. How do you think you would cope with an early losing run? Or, indeed, a winning one? Could you keep your composure? Are you comfortable with the prospect of betting long-term when you might have treated the game on a day-by-day basis in the past? Be realistic. Is the idea of professional gambling just an idle dream, albeit a pleasant one?

Hint 87: Professional gambling is a full-time job

In the summer of 1993, I attempted to merge my betting with my many other interests - and largely failed. Betting needs all your attention, quite probably for six days a week. You cannot expect to pick up the paper in the morning, with the expectation of finalising your selections by 11.00am in order to be on the golf course at noon. Taking an eight-hour day as a minimum and assuming you were betting purely off-course, you might expect to spend five hours studying form, an hour on the telephone to contacts and bookmakers, an hour watching the relevant races, and an hour reviewing the day's activities and planning for the next. Betting, as I have continually emphasised, is hard work - with the accent on the work. Being disciplined and dedicated does not mean you forfeit enjoyment from your betting; indeed, it is one of the main arguments in this book that such a considered approach actually facilitates enjoyment.

But not everybody would welcome having to stick to the above routine. For many, betting is an escape from everyday tedium and they enjoy the sense of spontaneity and freedom which it affords. For the professional, the rest of his life is his escape. With this in mind, it is essential for the professional punter to have a settled home life and almost certainly a number of interests to which he can turn to get away from the daily stress of betting. Those living alone are free to spend their evenings pouring over endless form books and videos - but others will have partners to consider. You might have good reasons for staking £500 on an 8-1 chance in a handicap at Ascot, but it will be four months' food money up in smoke to many others.

Get an office away from home if necessary - but do keep those close to you informed of your progress (without spending the entire evening ruminating over an unlucky loser in the last at Pontefract). A successful professional punter will have a high self-esteem allied to great powers of self-control, will be disciplined, alert and audacious, quick to spot the main chance and organised enough to take maximum advantage of it. The professional will be less a gambler than a successful money manager. Well-known writer and betting strategist Nick Mordin made a fascinating confession in his book *Betting For A Living*. "I don't like betting," wrote Mordin. "I hate the idea of handing over my hard-earned money to a bookmaker."

All of us should be able to identify with the second sentiment, if not the first. If losing itself were not bad enough, there is the added incentive of not boosting the ever-swelling funds of our friends on the other side of the counter. "Not liking betting," continues Mordin, "is the reason why I consistently make money in my betting. It is only when I've convinced myself that I simply must make a bet that I will do so. My instinct to sit out any race where I'm not absolutely sure a bet represents value saves me a fortune."

Patrick Veitch made a similar observation in a *Weekender* interview with Malcolm Heyhoe. "One of the major factors involved in betting is temperament. By that I mean the ability to judge each bet solely on its merits and not allow any decision to be affected by your recent performance." Clive Holt made a related point in an interview with Ian Carnaby in *Odds On* magazine. "You have to get used to losing, otherwise you'll never win. You've got to be able to weather a bad patch - and it comes down to strength of character. I'm frightened of losing, I don't want to fail." Sound advice indeed.

Personally, I would have admit that I do like betting - not just the form and statistical analysis, which is Nick's great strength, but also the act itself, with its adrenalin surges and all those feelings of agitation and expectation, which are betting's unmatchable thrills. This enjoyment can be dangerous, of course, not least because of the constant temptation to bet above one's means, perhaps in one frantic, all or nothing attempt to get it over with. Reading Anthony Holden's book *Big Deal: One Year As A Professional Poker Player*, I was fascinated by the number of times he was tempted to leave the rigours of the poker table and stake his all on an even-money chance at roulette.

The same kind of urge often comes upon me, just to keep staking and staking on one chosen horse in the hope of making some extraordinary, decisive breakthrough. And the only point in visiting the roulette table, as I see it, is to stake everything in one hit because the house percentage is sure to grind you into dust if you keep on playing. Just make sure your life-savings are not nestling in your wallet when you visit a casino! It reveals a good deal about Holden's temperament that he was able to forego the urge to stake all on red or black. Not for him Oscar Wilde's claim of being able to "resist anything except temptation".

Wilde would have made a terrible gambler, as proven by his reckless decision to take on the abominable Marquess Of Queensbury in the law courts, a decision which was to lead to his vilification and imprisonment. The gambler needs the strongest instinct for self-preservation, not Wilde's for self-destruction. Like other gamblers, I dislike losing, although I would qualify some of the above statements by saying that I can deal equably with almost all losses, providing I can satisfy myself that the bet struck was a sound one and that had I staked correctly. After all, we plan to win in the long run, not on every bet. We must be aware of our weaknesses and play to our strengths.

Socrates' famous maxim, to "know thyself", is one the gambler must take to heart. These days, I have cut down on the number of bets I strike. I have not always found it as easy as Nick Mordin to sit out a race, but it is something that must be done. When I back a horse, I do so to win a significant amount. This helps concentrate the mind. And every now and then, when I have a gut feeling that the right horse has come along, I go for the big, decisive win. Last season there were two attempts at glory. Basim, at 33-1 ante-post for the 2,000 Guineas, and How's Yer Father at 25-1 on the day for the Stewards Cup. Basim never got to post - but you have read about the How's Yer Father bet. His performance in finishing a close third helped underpin confidence in my ability to pull out the breakthrough winner, despite the lack of success in 1993.

As with so many activities, confidence is the key to betting. Confidence not just in our ability to pick winners, but the confidence that comes from knowing we have laid the ground rules for success. Now to methodology. I believe there are three different approaches to the business of professional gambling which you might like to consider. The three methods are sketched in (extremely) rough outline below.

Hint 88: The off-course method

As the title suggests, such backers will bet largely, or even exclusively, off-course. This approach will suit those backers who like to rely on their own opinions, gleaned from intensive form study. If you are to spend five or six hours a day studying and reviewing form, there will be little time left for travelling to and from the racecourse. They will enjoy working from home or an office environment and find the idea of spending time on the racecourse less attractive, perhaps feeling you have to waste too much time between races.

Such backers will rely upon their brain rather than their eye, or upon information, although they will study races to note significant performances and will have their contacts. A high proportion of their bets will be placed at early prices, thus negating a major reason for going racing. They may ask commission agents to place bets on their behalf, both on and off the course, because it is distinctly probable a number of their own accounts will have been closed or be subject to limitations. Their main problem for this type of backer will be overcoming the burden of betting tax, but they will save on petrol and admission costs to the racecourse.

Hint 89: The on-course method

Such backers will plan to spend a high proportion of their working day at, or travelling to, the racecourse, attending perhaps as many as four or five meetings a week. They will undertake form study but their methods will not be as painstaking as those of the off-course punter, due to pressure on time. They believe the information gained from being close to the action, notably by reviewing the well-being of horses in the paddock and by watching them canter to post, will help compensate for any deficiencies in form analysis. More importantly, there is the opportunity to bet tax-free, plus the chance to take full advantage of any value opportunities in the ring, notably by snapping up prices which will not be transmitted to the betting shops via SIS, having been available only on a couple of boards.

Such punters will enjoy the atmosphere on the racecourse and relish the cut and thrust of betting in the ring. They would probably feel isolated working purely from home. They will have to budget for transport and admission costs, and not be deterred by the prospect of a 100-mile drive home in the sleet after backing two heavy losers. Readers interested in the above method might like to read Nick Mordin's book *Betting For A Living*, which is crammed with Nick's thought-provoking and highly original, if idiosyncratic insights; and Clive Holt's long-established *Fineform* publications. Any book by the American gambler Andrew Beyer is worth reading, in particular his *My $50,000 Year At The Races*.

Hint 90: The contacts method

Such backers will adopt a markedly different approach to those discussed above, relying upon a network of contacts to mark their card and then interpreting the quality of the information and acting accordingly. Very little of their own time will be spent in close analysis of the form. They will prefer to rely on the views of trusted informants, who may be specialists in their field, notably in the compilation of betting forecasts, time figures or private handicaps.

This type of punter, who will probably have a business background, will also spend his time developing a network of contacts, with the aim of having a reliable source in each of the important yards, who will be able to brief him on the well-being of their horses. This punter will spend the morning gathering his information. A high proportion of his business will be done off-course, although he will probably spend some time on the racecourse, perhaps to liaise with and develop his contacts. Such punters will depend entirely upon their information feed but will be excellent money- as well as man-managers.

It should go without saying that all the above punters will realise that nothing is achieved in betting without constant adhesion to the value principle. Hopefully, even if you have no plans to consider betting for a living, the list will help you identify a method of betting which suits you. My preference is for the first of the three options, for I prefer to stick to my own opinions, and find it easier to switch off when betting from home. The prospect of a long journey back from the racecourse after a big loser is not one I relish, although there are few better feelings than to cheer your own horses home live. It will now be even clearer than it was at the outset that professional gambling is not to be approached lightly if it is to be approached at all. No wonder nearly all professionals diversify into tipping or some other means of selling their information. Any sensible businessman would. After all, if you are faced with a certain method of earning money, and an uncertain one, wouldn't you plump for the certainty?

Summary:

Nobody should consider betting for a living without making detailed plans regarding every aspect of their operation. There is a need to be realistic and professional gambling is a full-time job. There is, however, no reason why you should not aim to bet like a professional and to supplement your income or pension through betting.

part three
the top ten key hints

stage **ten**

the conclusion

This book has been something of a confession. I know the value of every single one of the hundred hints, for I have ignored them all in my time. This has not stopped me making a profit in financial terms over the years nor, on balance, from enjoying my betting - but it has detracted from that enjoyment and no doubt greatly reduced its profitability. Last summer was full of revelations for me, although largely not of my own choosing. My target was "to try to prove I could beat the system". On reflection, I am not sure I had spent sufficient time considering the implications of this statement. Of course it was necessary to win, in financial terms. This goes without saying. But I was also keen, as I wrote in my diary at the time, to 'expel the demons'.

Demons, I now realise, was nothing more than a (melo)dramatic term for bad habits. I listed a few of my bad habits in my diary at the beginning of the summer, including over-confidence and a predilection for wild staking. What I had not realised at the time was just how many more such habits had installed themselves at the heart of my betting over the years. Like me, you have probably gone through stages when you detested the whole betting business and wished to give it up for good. Perhaps during a losing run when it was all but impossible to imagine yourself ever backing a winner again.

There was this feeling that you were not in control, that the betting process dominated you, and not the other way around. Even the winners left you deflated, feeling you had not had enough on. It need not be so. After taking a breather from betting, I now feel a rare confidence for the future, full of the sense of vibrant anticipation I first felt when arriving at Warwick racecourse as a schoolboy truant in 1976, or when furtively pushing open the door of my local betting shop as an underage backer and striding in. Just think what might happen!

A backer's future is his to determine. Your future lies entirely in your own hands. Nobody can tell you which horses to back or how much to have on. Only you can decide. It is this feeling of autonomy, allied to the tremendous surge of excitement and freedom which comes from watching your horse perform to expectations, which has always attracted me to betting and attracts me still.

Jeffrey Bernard once commented that there were only two matters to be addressed before striking a bet: "My main, and foremost question has usually been - Is fate, God, luck and love on my side? The second such question has usually been - can I win enough money on such and such a horse to avoid actual work?" You will have your own reasons for betting, but it is my guess they will true to the spirit, if not the letter, of Bernard's observation.

This book, when it comes down to it, has been about clearing away the clutter in order that fate, God and luck are on our side. And we will certainly be betting to a purpose, perhaps to win enough to avoid work (my aim from the age of 15), but certainly to gain an increased measure of enjoyment and satisfaction from an activity which so often promises the world, only to deliver little or nothing at all. It is possible to win and to win well at betting and now is the time to go out and prove it. I leave you with 10 final hints, by way of summary.

Hint 91: Start with a clean sheet

The best way to get a perspective on your betting is to take a breather. Not just one of a day or so, but one stretching into weeks, even months. Spend the time analysing your betting. Don't just curse the losers, and the bad bets, but pat yourself on the back for the winners, and the shrewd wagers which left you with a sense of inner satisfaction after you placed them. Then, when you return to the action, make sure you capitalise upon your insights. Keep reminding yourself not to fall back into the bad habits which have so often dragged you down.

Hint 92: Don't be in a hurry to bet

Having started with a clean sheet, try to keep one. Not all bets will be winners, of course, but make sure you can look back upon each and every one with satisfaction. Always work through each bet stage by stage. First the form analysis, then the price assessment, then the staking. Only bet when you are convinced you are doing the right thing. If in doubt, stay out.

Hint 93: Find an edge

Your review of your past betting performance will have helped reveal when you are at your most confident. It will come as no surprise that, for me, these feelings come when I am backing horses trained by Dick Hern. Over the years I have followed the stable so closely I have been able to form deep convictions about certain horses winning particular races. They have not always succeeded, but the bets have been among my most memorable and enjoyable. Maybe you will decide to choose your own stable to follow or maybe to concentrate upon a certain type of bet - perhaps the Tote Placepot. Then there is the choice between Flat and Jumps, handicaps and non-handicaps, big fields and small fields. The list could go on endlessly. But try to specialise and don't be swayed by outside opinions. The greatest satisfaction in betting comes from watching a horse you have picked out and backed on your own behalf come steaming home ahead of its field.

Hint 94: Bet to strengths

Most punters are stuck in a vicious circle. On the whole, they do what everybody else does - and what everybody else does, on the whole, is lose. We will not be following the herd by backing poor value favourites or by latching on to useless gossip masquerading as inside information. We will be betting to strengths. Our strengths. Strength and confidence are intertwined in betting. Make sure you bet where and when you want and nowhere else. And stick to your guns. Dick Hern enjoyed some lean and terrible seasons in the mid- to late-1980s and lost the loyalty of those who should have known better. But those who stuck with him were magnificently rewarded with Nashwan in 1989 - 2,000 Guineas day, in particular, is one I shall never forget, the highlight of my betting life, and there was added spice in the sense of being vindicated after so many years of struggle.

Hint 95: Try to back horses who have an outstanding winning chance and who represent value for money.

I have always been attracted by the big outsider, the one-bet, one-winner scenario which can change your life. While still holding to this ideal, I now realise that I have been backing too many speculative outsiders. Not enough emphasis can be placed upon the hints to give preference to recent form and to try to follow momentum horses. Too often last summer I was striking theoretical value bets on horses who could win on their best form but were probably no longer up to it. I think it is essential to believe your horse has an outstanding winning chance as well as representing value for money.

The second criteria, of course, is a pre-requisite for any bet. This does not mean we should limit ourselves only to rock-solid odds-on shots, although I shall not deter you if this is your chosen strategy - although you must bet purely on-course, for the tax will undermine you completely in the shops. It is the confidence point again. There are times when we really believe in a horse. The more we think about it the more excited we become. These are the bets. Macs Maharanee and How's Yer Father would qualify from among those bets discussed in this book. The latter was a 25-1 shot. If all our bets were as good as these we could not fail.

Hint 96: If you must bet, have a proper bet

When I was 14, and commencing what one hesitates to describe as a career in betting, I read some advice along the above lines. It has taken me 18 years and my worst-ever season for me to fully appreciate the wisdom contained in the statement. There is no point in striking a bet if it is not going to make any difference to your life. This is one of the traps many punters fall into. They have backed scores of winners - but they have not made any difference, not in the long run. We should aim to care about every bet we strike, to feel we would be losing something important to us were we to be deprived of it. Hardly any of the small, just for fun bets will come into this category. Patience is again the key. Wait for the good bets to come along, the ones which get you tingling with excitement and anticipation, the ones you strike with a feeling of 'all guns blazing'. These horses, these proper bets, invariably run well if they do not win. Wait for them and wait some more. Then pounce. Every time you bet have a real bet, a proper bet - don't fiddle around.

Hint 97: Stake consistently

This is one of the most important hints in the book and bears repeating.

Inconsistent and ill-considered staking can destroy all the hard work undergone in form study and value assessment. It is simply not good enough to have a big bet on a horse one day and a small bet on an identical selection the next. Mood often dictates here, but do your utmost not to let it. If you do not feel fully in control about a bet, if you are not sure how much you should be having on, leave it alone.

Remember our punter with a hangover in hint six, striking bets he would soon come to regret. This is all of us at some time - perhaps too much of the time. Analyse your bets. Try the level-stakes test to see if this method might suit you. But always aim to stake consistently, one day to the next. By all means raise your stakes if your bank is growing but do so slowly and sensibly.

Hint 98: Bet to a purpose

We will all have set ourselves realistic profit targets, to which each winner will contribute, thus rendering it part of a coherent strategy, instead of a random event. Aiming to achieve this profit target, or making a worthy attempt at achieving it, should imbue us with a sense of purpose about our betting. Most punters bet randomly, to no discernible purpose. Nap selections are understaked and any winnings are quickly handed back on indiscriminate selections. Very few punters win in the long run. To do so is a notable achievement, of which you can be justifiably proud. Our broad purpose is to win and win well. Never lose sight of this and do not let your bookmaker off the hook. He does not deserve it.

Hint 99: Be sensibly ambitious

I am convinced that everybody could quickly improve their betting by at least 25 per cent if they removed some of their worst bad habits. But it is important to be realistic, especially when setting profit targets. Do not expect to turn into the next Alex Bird overnight, nor aim to be sipping Barcardi on a Caribbean island by the turn of the year. Winning takes time. The skills required for successful form study and value assessment cannot be learned overnight. I have not shirked from laying emphasis on hard work in this book for no other reason than there is no avoiding it.

Think long-term and plan to a sensible goal. Do not become deflated if you make only limited progress at the outset. Keep analysing and learning from your bets. Watch for patterns emerging. Get to know a stable over a year or two.

Refine your technique on the Placepot and other favourite bets. Be sensibly ambitious. Eventually things will begin to turn - and when they do, you will not regret the wait, believe me.

Hint 100: Make the most of your betting

Only the bookmakers are narrow-minded enough to believe betting is purely about the money. It is also a means to self-knowledge and self-realisation. In a famous essay entitled *Where The Action Is*, the sociologist Erving Goffman outlined how he believes gambling offers the individual opportunities to display courage, gameness, integrity (through the maintenance of discipline under pressure), gallantry (by being a good loser), composure, dignity, presence of mind and self-confidence. How different from the stereotype of the gambler as the downcast loser and the eternal sufferer! The bookmakers may conspire against us at every turn but it is possible to buck the system. After all, if systems are not there to be bucked, what can they possibly be for?